Water and What We Know

Water and What We Know

Following the Roots of a Northern Life

KAREN BABINE

University of Minnesota Press
Minneapolis • London

Grateful acknowledgment is made for permission from Jonathan
Johnson to reprint excerpts from "The Last Great Flood" and "Three
Hours out of Fairbanks" from *Mastodon, 80% Complete,* by Jonathan
Johnson (Pittsburgh: Carnegie Mellon University Press, 2001).

Published by the University of Minnesota Press
111 Third Avenue South, Suite 290
Minneapolis, MN 55401–2520
http://www.upress.umn.edu

Library of Congress Cataloging-in-Publication Data
Babine, Karen.
[Essays. Selections]
Water and what we know : following the roots of a northern life /
Karen Babine.
ISBN 978-0-8166-9678-9 (pb: acid-free paper)
Title. PS3602.A2314A6 2015
814'.6—dc23   2014035383

Printed in the United States of America on acid-free paper

The University of Minnesota is an equal-opportunity educator and
employer.

21 20 19 18 17 16 15   10 9 8 7 6 5 4 3 2 1

Dedicated to the memory and legacy of
Kermit and Phyllis Kleene

CONTENTS

In This Place, on This Day

It's mid-May, just after the fishing opener in northern Minnesota, and I am sitting on the couch in front of the big picture window, feet propped on an ancient ottoman, cup of tea at my elbow. It is Tea Time at the Lake, that sacred time after Afternoon Naps. My grandparents, who built the Cabin the summer my mother was pregnant with me, taught us to think in Proper Nouns. If my grandparents were here, my grandmother would be filling her teapot and finding the *kluntjes,* the German white sugar rock candy. But I am alone, drinking my tea out of my grandfather's mug, the one with the violin on it. The chainsaw-carved bald eagle that was their fiftieth anniversary present from our family hangs on the wall, the only decoration on the knotty pine. The trees haven't quite filled in the spaces between the picture window and Third Crow Wing Lake, but there is enough green in different shapes and textures to make me dizzy, the round birch leaves shimmering like coins in the afternoon light.

Yesterday, I walked down to the lake and found several baby white pine trees, and I put a few fallen branches around them so they would not be stepped on or mowed over. "Oh!" my mother exclaimed when I told her of my finds. "You found some Kermit Trees!" Kermit was my grandfather, a farmer by blood, a vocational agriculture teacher by trade, and a conservationist at heart, gone since 2006. The land of his blood, the southwestern Minnesota prairie settled by his grandfather in the immediate aftermath of the 1862 U.S.–Dakota War that banished the Minnesota Dakota from the state, was largely treeless. My grandmother, still alive and cracking jokes at her assisted living facility, was a history and English teacher, but she also came from farming blood and a conservationist ethic, especially when it came to trees. My grandfather would find baby white pines and put a stake next to them to mark them. He would water them and transplant them when they got big enough. Growing up this way, I thought I knew the trees of Third Crow Wing and the Cabin fairly well, but I learned recently that the summer the Cabin was built a fire went through the Badoura State Forest just to the east of here, and much of the pine that frames the Cabin came from trees damaged by the fire. Third Crow Wing continues to surprise me, reminding me that there are still more stories here, in this place I know better than anywhere else in the world, than I can ever hope to know, and I enjoy the humility of knowing the natural world doesn't need me to create meaning.

Last week I considered putting satellite Internet out here for the summer, but the service providers who came out to inspect the property said there was only one spot for a dish—we're too far out for cable—and it would require taking out a tree, a straggly little oak that wasn't even on our property. "Well," my mother said, "they obviously weren't raised on the sacredness of trees!" I decided to forgo the Internet because it wasn't worth the tree's life.

The world here is blue, and it is green. It has been a long time since I have been able to spend extended time in this world, my life since college planting me in worlds of blue and gold, prairies and grasslands and cornfields rather than trees and lakes. But every place I have lived during those years has asked me to find the value and the specific in where I am, to find the local knowledge of how to live in that place, what makes that place unlike any other place. *What does it mean to live in this place, on this particular day? What do we see when we look?* Where I sit right now, I have returned to the world of water, in Hubbard County, Minnesota, which boasts ninety lakes in a ten-mile radius. The loons sing me to sleep in twilight that lasts forever, and they scream me awake in the morning.

But there is more here, and it is not always comfortable—and it shouldn't be.

As I watch the white caps on Third Crow Wing, I know that this water has a relationship with the land that contains it. Last night I watched the thunderheads roll across the lake from the west, and I hoped that the rain would be soft, not torrential, because the farmers need a good soaking rain. The soil here is sugar sand, hugely problematic when it comes to erosion but perfect soil for potatoes and strawberries and edible beans. This summer, I will drive to Keske's U-Pick and buy flats of strawberries to freeze for the winter. I have images in my head of taking my two-year-old niece Cora with me and laughing as she stains every inch of herself with as many strawberries as she can pick, just as my sisters and I did when we were little. I remember going out as a kid with the little old ladies of the church my father served in Nevis, gleaning potatoes for *lefse* in the fall. As I drive Highway 87 from the Cabin toward Park Rapids, through the little town of Hubbard, the fields are already planted, the turkey manure from local turkey farms spread and tilled into the soil, the center-pivot irrigation systems naked like dinosaur skeletons. There used to be signs that warned of "Irrigation Overspray," but they have long since disappeared, about the same time that my middle sister learned that the signs did not say "Injured Osprey."

The idea of an ethic of place is more complicated to me than a simple land ethic, a philosophy that, in the words of Aldo Leopold in *Nature's Services,* "changes the role of *Homo sapiens* from conqueror of the land community to plain member and citizen of it." Such a position statement—in the sense of literal positioning of a human being in relation to what surrounds it—is important, and I agree with Leopold. But an ethic of place is larger and respects the larger complexities: it is made up of land and soil composition and geology, water in all its forms, history, culture, personal experience, and everything else that makes up the lens we have constructed to understand the world around us. Location is a spot on a map. Place is context, everything you bring to a location.

Perhaps one might consider the difference between a land ethic and a place ethic as *time.* As much as I might imagine North Dakota free of the Oil Patch, the effect of the Oil Patch is larger than the land itself: I recently read that workers in the Oil Patch are being killed at five times the national rate, and North Dakota has made it less costly for companies to pay death benefits to the families than to institute safety regulations. Mining is historically associated with the Iron Range in Minnesota, so close to the pristine Boundary Waters and the western edge of Lake Superior. Place means knowing that there is a fine line between the negative effects of that mining on the environment and the reality that people need jobs to feed their families. An ethic of place seeks to understand the complexities that humans bring to a landscape; it is not as simple as turning the Great Plains back into prairie.

Place means more than knowledge. For example, it requires understanding the contrast between living in Hubbard County with sand for soil and living in Fargo–Moorhead with clay; there is a difference between what the 1997 Red River flood meant for Fargo and what it meant for Grand Forks. My Air Force friend Tom's experience is another example. He had moved from Nebraska, where we had known each other, to Washington, D.C., to work at the Pentagon. I asked him about the earthquake that hit the East Coast in August 2011. As a recent transplant from the Midwest to the East Coast, he hadn't been bothered much, he said, but on Facebook and Twitter, the West Coast mocked the East Coast's strong reaction to what they considered a tiny earthquake, barely worthy of the name. The last time the earth had moved like that at the Pentagon, a plane had crashed into the outer rings of the building.

This is place.

An ethic of place requires a certain level of discomfort. I know that the land settled by my mother's family, the Swedes in Chisago County and the Germans in Chippewa County, is stolen land. They took advantage of the Homestead Acts and the Dawes Act, and I don't know how to feel about this. Certainly my ancestors did not feel conflicted, but there is no answer to *What do I do about it now?* Everywhere I have lived is stolen land. How does one reconcile the wrongs committed by a settler culture with what it means to live in this place on this day? I do not know, and part of my developing ethic of place is to explore what makes me uncomfortable.

I keep coming back to the near-universal sacredness of trees, which has become a cultural tree fetish, and the sanctity of water and what we have done to the landscape by wanting it to be something other than what it is by writing a history on it that claims to be the One True Story. The prairie that my German ancestors settled, left behind after the Glacial Lake Agassiz retreated, is not supposed to have trees, and it is not supposed to be farmland. It is supposed to be grassland, a place that needs roots six feet deep. This Land of 10,000 Lakes has a complicated relationship with water, but it is not alone in this—so do the lands of blue and gold—and the essays here work through a complicated relationship of water and soil, of fire and water, of people and place, because it is never as simple as black or white—most of the time it is both. These essays wonder how those stories come to be written, how humans can read the stories of the landscape and the stories of how we move through that landscape. These essays exercise what I consider to be *an* ethic of place to find the universal in my specific, to attempt to reconcile what cannot be fully understood or rectified. *What does it mean to live in this place on this day?* What can we know by looking more specifically at what surrounds us, and what can we never know, no matter how hard we try?

I know that the trees around the Cabin are second growth, filling in the landscape after the precious white pines were logged off a hundred years ago and sent to places like Chicago. The trees of Hubbard County tell one story of the place, just as the lakes do. When I drive through Park Rapids, there is a bare spot in the middle of town where, a year ago, a microburst tornado took down a stand of Norway pines—leaving everything else around it intact—and there is a story there, too. Stories can be lost, but they can also be replanted, transplanted. It is important to be able to read the stories when there are no voices to tell them, to find the Kermit trees. On Memorial Day my grandfather was the only one to stand when the Coast Guard hymn was played. Now there is no one. But his trees are still here.

Roald Amundsen's Teeth

I tasca State Park is everything that is right with the world. The root of its name is *veritas caput,* Latin for "true head," the name formed of the last three letters of the first word and the first two letters of the second, and this place marks more than the headwaters of the Mississippi River in northern Minnesota. When I am away from the North Woods, I feel like my lungs can never fully inflate, and when I get back here, to Hubbard County, I feel like I can finally breathe.

The world here is green, but it isn't so much the variety of colors of green that make Itasca—and northern Minnesota, for that matter—what it is. It's the textures of green, from the lace of ferns to the spikes of pine needles to the poison ivy leaves at your ankles to the birch leaves overhead. Green in Minnesota is more than a color and more than textures. Green becomes the color of light; it becomes the taste in your mouth when you wake up in the morning and step outside your camper; it becomes a sound. You might be able to discern the individual sounds of wind in the leaves and loon calls, but together the sound is simply *green*. Green is what you wrap yourself in when you go to sleep, regardless of the actual color of your bedding; green is the warmth of the electric blanket, the cool and damp of the air coming in through the cracked window above you. Green is what you sprinkle over your morning cereal, what you add to your coffee or tea. And when you leave, green becomes the color of the shadow that follows you home.

In Nebraska, I fight the itch to be in the North, to put the Jeep in drive and head north on I-29. It's not just my home in Hubbard County that I want, the roads and trees and waters that are mine, but the state of mind that is purely Northern, a kind of Proper Noun concept. These days I only get Up North twice a year, but my desire to be where the trees and the lakes and the license plates and the accents are recognizable can be staggering. This isn't a desire for home—it is something else. Matsuo Basho, the seventeenth-century Japanese poet and essayist, went North—a literal north, northern Japan—because as Nobuyuki Yuasa writes in the introduction to his 1966 translation of Basho's *The Narrow Road to the Deep North*, "The North was largely unexplored territory, and it represented for Basho all the mystery there was in the universe." This, I want to believe, is why people left the East Coast, to find a place where nothing was figured out. Realistically, I know that the first mass migration out of New England happened as a result of the 1816 Year without Summer, a catastrophic climate change caused by the 1815 eruption of Mount Tambora in Indonesia, when the temperatures were so cold that nothing grew and people moved west to avoid starvation. I want to ascribe a mythology to the movement, to think that just as the mental East is the opposite of West, North is the antidote to the

South. But the truth is that we have to leave our comfort zones to find where we are uncomfortable. True North cannot be found sitting in an armchair.

I would like to believe in the literal sense of American place mythology: a compilation of origin stories to explain how we came to be where we are, how we came to be who we are. But in the sense of an origin story, our place mythologies are supposed to break down when we get closer. We tell ourselves that the North is a place of desire, that the North is both place and compass direction, a place and a destination, a place and an idea. A place where thought and action have been pared down to their essences, a place that drew its mythology in watercolors, and it is a lovely idea to consider. The Minnesota essayist Paul Gruchow, in his award-winning book *Boundary Waters,* an exploration of the preserved wilderness in northeast Minnesota that borders Canada, observes,

> Our cabin faced north. How many things in this
> country pointed north: the river, the winds, the
> tops of the tallest trees, the limbs of the windblown
> trees, the thickest bark on the trees. North was the
> only direction. Americans have been preoccupied
> with the mystique of the west, but the north has
> also had its powerful pull on us. . . . The allure of
> the north, of the west, is the allure of elsewhere.

I have, on many occasions, stood on the banks of the Red River of the North, the border between Moorhead, Minnesota, and Fargo, North Dakota. I like to see how the river rises and retreats from its banks, allowing the clay to form deep cracks that are never quite dry or solid. For most of my college career, the Red was an arthritic snake, slowly moving its thick body north from its headwaters to Lake Winnipeg. Slow, steady, eternal. North. Always North. The Red knew its direction was more important than that of the Mississippi, whose headwaters were thirty miles from my hometown. North was the important direction—and sometimes the Red forcibly reminded us of the direction we should go. The 1997 Flood was the most potent reminder, but our ideas of One-Hundred-Year Floods were reenvisioned in 2001 and 2006, and in 2009 the water surpassed even 1997 levels in Fargo. The only direction we could look was North.

These are the stories we tell ourselves, the stories we should recognize as just stories—but somewhere along the way, we have turned mythology into fact. No matter the latitude and longitude, we tell ourselves—and believe—that North is where the boundary between person and place is thrown down and true freedom finds its native soil. This is the root of the desire for North, the point from which everything else grows, but it is the change in perspective here that is important, not the compass direction on its own merits. It's the difference between the Mercator projection map and the Peters projection (so delightfully considered in an episode of *The West Wing*)—the difference between a map that inflates the area of countries the farther they are from the equator and a map that shows the area of countries accurately—and how we equate North and South with good and bad, with civilized and uncivilized, with light and dark. All the maps point North—even if we put the northern hemisphere on the bottom half of the map. It is a choice that has specific cultural effects, even in the Minnesota North Woods.

The North, as an idea, represents absolute, pure desire to pursue an ideal, Nietzsche's "true climate," the place where the "exact geographical location—corresponds to the 'climate' of the thinker." The desire overrules caution and risks everything, including life and death and the closure of being buried in a marked place. Desire is the invisible force of the mythological North, but it is the part we comprehend most clearly. We understand it, even if we don't know what it is we are desiring. Someday I would like to see the polar bears at Churchill and then go even farther to cross the Arctic Circle, but there is a significant part of me that is happy with the North I find in Minnesota. This summer, we took my niece to the National Eagle Center in Wabasha, Minnesota, where she met four bald eagles and one golden eagle. The five eagles are permanently disabled—mostly from vehicle collisions—and Cora fell in love with the thirteen-year-old named Columbia. When we left Harriet, the thirty-three-year-old female featured on Minnesota's veteran's license plate, I wanted to see the slice of her black wings against the cold grayness of the sky above the Mississippi River, flowing past the Eagle Center. On the October Sunday Gram died, I was driving from Minneapolis to Fargo and saw an eagle riding the thermals above the interstate highway. I would like to believe that eagles carry the spirit of my grandmother, who loved them. I don't need to go to Alaska—a place she counted among her favorites—to see eagles.

It isn't that I don't desire to hook up my camper to the Jeep and hit the road, to find *elsewhere,* because I do, but I find that the closer I get to places in Minnesota, the less I understand about this place I have called home. I do not have to increase my distance to see new things in this place I think I know: I simply need to look closer, look differently, to shift what I want to see when I look. The Latin root of *desire* means *star*—which both further mystifies and demystifies the North: a longing for something that will always remain out of reach but by which the world is understandable, navigable. The stars are stories: they are the animals of the Zodiac if you imagine hard enough; stars are how we find our way home.

So it was, I imagine, for Roald Amundsen. In the archives of my alma mater, Concordia College, two of his teeth gather dust. I saw them once. In 1927, Amundsen was in Moorhead, just a stone's throw from the Red River, giving a lecture. He developed a toothache and visited a local dentist, who removed two teeth. A year later, Amundsen disappeared in the Arctic while searching for survivors of a downed airship. In the 1930s, the teeth were donated to the college. The two teeth are all that is left of his unexplainable desire to go North, a tangible reminder of the required physical, mental, and emotional risks in the North where everything is worth that risk.

In the North, the sun is of art and science and religion. The lure of northern light—not specifically the aurora borealis—is not necessarily wanting to be out of the darkness, but wanting to find the brilliant moments. At the extremes of the North, the land of the midnight sun is of a world all its own, though I have never seen it for myself. The winter white sunlight is both the absence of all colors and the presence of all colors. Summer sunlight is yellow and contains its own specific properties. In the winter, you have sun dogs, those rainbow parentheses around the sun that are the result of sunlight shattered by ice crystals. Even the science of parhelia—sun dogs—is related to this land-based mythology of the North: in more southerly climes, they are rare enough that residents do not know what they are. When I lived in Ohio, people didn't know what I was talking about; living in Nebraska, I have never seen them. While living in Fargo during this last winter, which regularly saw minus-forty-degree wind-chills, I saw sun dogs nearly every day.

In the North, the sun dogs bark, chase their tails in excitement, and lead us *elsewhere*.

The mythology of the North would have us believe that North America is a land of desire. Without desire, we would not have crossed the land bridge in the west; we would not have sailed the seas from the east. It is this desire that forms the basis of the mythologies of our American landscapes. Kevin McMahon writes in *Arctic Twilight: Reflections on the Destiny of Canada's Northern Land and People,* "Every country has its mythological territories. America has the rugged west. Britain has the glorious Sea. Canada has the Arctic, the glistening white vessel of our sanctimonious soul. The national halo. The image itself has the ability to conjure innocence, cleanse." Mythology is larger than real life because it is not real life. Mythology is, by its very nature, created. And so as Europeans settled the continent, we created our own origin stories based on what we wanted to find. We want home from the Heartland, freedom from the West, culture and gentility from the South, and mental clarity from the North, so we created myths that offered the settlers a new history where they had had none. It is not as simple as political treaties, land for sale from foreign governments, land stolen from indigenous tribes. The landscape itself dictates what stories will be told of it, the creation myths of the place. It is Paul Bunyan and Nanabozho, the Anishinaabe trickster—and in a later story, Nanabozho kills Paul Bunyan, which is interesting in itself.

In *This Cold Heaven,* Gretel Ehrlich writes, "I learned that treeline can be a factor of latitude, not just altitude—it is a biological boundary created by the cold—and came to think of the treeless polar north as the top of a mountain lying on its side." What if the treeline isn't just latitude and altitude, but also attitude? What if the treeline is metaphorical, not literal? I consider this because Minnesota becomes consistently thicker with trees the farther north one goes. It is this treeless mentality I want to consider, where there is nothing to break the mental horizon. No mosquitoes to slap, no humans around to disturb the mind.

The stories that come out of this desire are reactions to the landscape: if we wanted stories of realistic life, we would stay in our suburban split-levels or our studio apartments, content with our nine-to-five jobs and chauffeuring the kids to soccer games. Because of this reality, the land-based mythology exists in the literal human sphere as well as the emotional. We want to hear stories of people doing things we don't have the guts to do. I want to go to Alaska, but I'm glad I'm not the first one moving in that direction. I read Gary Paulsen's book on the Iditarod because I don't want to run it myself. Those of northern mythologies are in search of the ever elusive *more,* Gruchow's *elsewhere.* More is always tricky. There is always something better, something stronger, something more beautiful. There is never an end to *more,* not even at the edge of the world. There is always one *more* step to be taken. And the lure of that next step is intoxicating to some.

Winter in Minnesota is beautiful. There's no denying that. I drove today from Detroit Lakes to Park Rapids on Highway 34. It's late in December, and these are some of my favorite miles in the world. The sky is pewter-blue gray, only a shade or two lighter than the asphalt under my tires. Hoarfrost from the overnight still covers the trees. Green gray. Blue gray. Silver. Pure white. Symphony of gray on gray on white. The sun breaks through the cloud cover, adding white, cool light. Then the light goes back into the thick gray cotton batting of clouds overhead. When I reach Park Rapids—a forty-five-mile journey—I want to turn around and go back, just to enjoy the drive again. It's a lateral drive, west to east, but it gets me closer to where I want to be.

North seems like an escape. North implies less population and development, the blessing of solitude. North suggests a place not touched by humans. North hints at a simplicity of thought and actions, of color schemes and sounds. Sometimes the implications are based in reality, and sometimes they are just dreams, something we would like to find if only we could get out of the milieu that ties us down. We want our mythological Norths to be cold, because cold removes the undesirables. Who can think through the noise of tourists and Jet Skis? And how can you truly appreciate milder temperatures without first going through the hardship of below-zero temperatures? In *The Singing Wilderness,* Minnesota essayist Sigurd F. Olson writes, "To anyone who has spent a winter in the north and known the depths to which the snow can reach, known the weeks when the mercury stays below zero, the first hint of spring is a major event. You must live in the north to understand it. You cannot just come up for it as you might go to Florida for the sunshine and the surf. To appreciate it, you must go through considerable enduring." Enduring the North means a time frame of weeks, or even months, when the only echo you can find is the wind off the ice.

More than the presence of something, the mythology of North is an absence of speech. At its core, isn't part of the desire for North strongly flavored with the desire to escape human voices? One of the largest pet peeves of those who live in northern Minnesota is the tendency for the hordes of Twin Cities tourists to buy up lake property, clog the lakes with Jet Skis, drive up the property values—and then loudly complain about the taxes and refuse to support the schools. I want them to go away, or at least be quiet enough to listen to the place that drew them away from the Cities. When writing of the shrine at the summit of Mount Nikko, Basho does not desecrate the shrine by speaking more than is required, even on paper: after describing the necessary history, Basho writes, "To say more about the shrine would be to violate its holiness." Contemplating the holiness of such a place is best done internally, and if not strictly within the confines of the writer's mind or heart, then on the page, not in conversation with other humans.

In *The Singing Wilderness,* Olson writes of disturbing that silence as a sacrilege: "At times on quiet waters one does not speak aloud but only in whispers, for then all noise is sacrilege" and "There is a moment of suspense when the quiet can be felt, when it presses down on everything and to speak seems a sacrilege. Suddenly the air is white with drifting flakes and the tension is gone." Silence in the wild is something to be savored because it is more than a mere absence of sound. Silence in the wild North is not always the absence of sound but the wind in the trees, chattering squirrels, singing birds. To use your own voice, to introduce human sound into that melody, is to destroy the natural sound. If you are speaking, then the birds and the squirrels are not. Perhaps that is the root of Olson's sacrilege. In Robert Hass's *20th Century Pleasures,* a chapter comparing jazz and poetry called "Listening and Making" fits into Olson's ideas of silence and sacrilege. Hass writes, "This can be hypnotically peaceful; it can also be terrifying, to come so near to self-abandonment, to whatever in ourselves wants to stay there in that sound, rocking and weeping, comforted."

But language in the North has come to serve more than one purpose—and it should never function to fill the silence. The Greenlanders tell of the baby giant Sila, who controls the weather. Gretel Ehrlich writes, "In Greenland, *sila* means both weather and consciousness." This linguistic turn cannot be accidental. If we Minnesotans do not know what to say, we talk about the weather, mostly because it dictates so much of our lives. If the mythology of the North requires that the land be open enough to allow stories to expand to fill the place, shouldn't we expect that the language of the North do the same? Instead, the language condenses, doubles in on itself, opens a door so wide that worlds can pass through, shoulder to shoulder.

That door opened this morning, light spilled through, that cool white light of a northern morning that is brighter for the snow, and I was momentarily blinded. In Ehrlich's *The Future of Ice,* she writes, "The Japanese word *oku* means not only 'north,' but also 'deep,' 'inner,' 'the inner heart of the mountain,' 'to penetrate to the depth of something or someone,' 'the bottom of one's heart,' and 'the end of one's mind.'" It was one of those moments where the misty nebula of thought and logic and unnamed yearning and half-felt desire solidified into something tangible, something you can hold in your hand, something that glows with life and heat and everything you didn't know you needed but now can't imagine living without. This kind of moment is like a shot of adrenaline to your heart, to your head, to your nerve endings, sharpening your eyes, your awareness, to the point where clarity becomes painful. In that one word, *oku,* is summed up everything that the North is, not just what Basho was searching for in his "Narrow Road to the Deep North." Basho is not only moving toward the compass direction of north but also traveling into the deep North, the point where his internal boundaries are no longer ambiguous. *We should all be so lucky,* I thought, stunned—in the truest sense of the word—and I was ready to pack up, put the Jeep in drive, and search for Sila, in search of *oku,* in search of all that I would not find in my southern climes of Nebraska. The lure of understanding—of more—was thrilling.

It was the mental equivalent of standing outside on a clear winter night in northern Minnesota. Summer nights, with a twilight that lasts forever, do not offer the same clarity. Even winter days do not. On these nights, you're intensely glad to be alive, just for the pleasure of breathing. Inhale, exhale. There are some nights when it's too cold to breathe, when breathing feels like inhaling crushed glass, too cold to stand outside for longer than you have to. But on those rare nights when the temperature is between ten and thirty degrees, when the wind is still, breathing becomes one of life's most important gifts, and you can't quite figure out why. Breathing during the summer is a different kind of pleasure, when it's not so much about breathing as it about stars and northern lights and mosquitoes. Breathing during the winter is about air, about stillness, about darkness and brightness, about other things.

Gruchow, better than most, understands the way the language of the North works. At the end of a brief narrative in *Boundary Waters,* explaining how he arrived at Isle Royale, the largest island in Lake Superior, he concludes, "[Some] places can be claimed but never conquered, assayed but never fathomed, essayed but never explained." Beyond the encounter of human and place, Gruchow uses his language to try to articulate this place, like *oku* and *sila,* meshing "assay" and "essay." The crux of this passage is that the root of *fathom,* from Old English, means "outstretched arms." Since the average man's armspan is six feet, the length given to the measurement of a fathom, this is absolutely the appropriate verb for the North: if a place is going to apprehend a person—if that Northern winter is going to hold me in place—what better way to do that than with welcoming, outstretched arms? If we can't touch, how will we ever know the place? How will we find our true climate, the *more* we are looking for, if we don't stand still long enough to know?

The Inheritance of Apples

Picture this: a simple knotty pine–paneled cabin in northern Minnesota, on a lake called Third Crow Wing. In the kitchen, an open room, the counters are white and the cupboards are dark brown. The floors are carpeted in colors unique to the 1970s.

A man, his age somewhere between sixty and seventy, sits at the old oak kitchen table that had belonged to his wife's parents. There's a good story behind that table and chairs, but that's for another time. In one hand, he holds a half-stripped Granny Smith apple. In the other hand, he holds a vegetable peeler. Under his hands is a pie tin with a pile of long, thin green apple peelings. He thinks that the peeler is getting dull and they'll have to replace it, but with characteristic Depression-era thrift, he decides that because it still mostly works there's no good reason to throw it away. In any case, he is able to peel the apple in one long strip. This pleases him, and he shows his wife when she turns around.

A woman, about the same age, stands at the counter. She cuts cold shortening into flour, then adds vinegar and water. She mixes only as much as is necessary; if she handles the shortening too much, it will start to warm, and she wants to avoid that. The secret to her famous piecrust—even as her Swedish modesty dismisses the notion—is in the temperature of the shortening and water. They need to be cold. If the water is too warm, it starts to melt the shortening, and the crust won't be light and flaky. She divides the dough with practiced ease, then rolls out the piecrust on her pastry cloth to fit her pie tin.

There is no conversation between them. He measures out his words much the same way his wife measures out ingredients for her pies: carefully and precisely. His wife is mostly deaf, even with her hearing aids. Sometimes she'll sing the hymns and Swedish songs of her childhood or chatter without really expecting a reaction from him, but being hard of hearing himself (and too stubborn to wear his hearing aid) he doesn't hear much of what she says. In any case, they have been married for so long that words often seem superfluous.

She moves to her husband to gather the apples. He peels the apples just fine, she thinks, but he hasn't quite mastered how she wants them cut, even after so many years. But she grins at his peeling of the apple in one piece. She loads the pie tin until it overflows. No need to be stingy with the apples or with the sugar. She knows she won't get a good pie by being stingy with the apples or the sugar. A full cup of sugar, maybe more, depending on the apples. She chews on one of the pieces and decides they're perfect. If they were a little less crisp or tart, she'd add some lemon juice. She adds little pats of butter so things won't burn.

She places the top crust over the apples and uses a

fork to press the sides closed, then pokes air holes in the top. The pie goes in the oven. She'll cut up the leftover crust, sprinkle some cinnamon and sugar on top of the pieces, and bake them too, so she and her husband can have a little something sweet with their tea. Unless, of course, her granddaughters are visiting, and then instead she'll use the leftover crust to make a little turnover apple pie for them. Her granddaughters love her pies almost as much as her son-in-law does.

Almost.

In the early 1960s, my grandparents managed an apple orchard near New Ulm in southern Minnesota. Both of them came from farming families, but they were not farmers themselves. My grandfather had gone to college at the University of Minnesota, but when World War II broke out, he took his newly married brother's place in the draft, allowing Leonard to remain on the family farm. After the war, after my grandparents met, married, and had my mother, they went back to the university, and my grandfather used G.I. Bill education benefits to get his master's degree in agricultural economics. He taught vocational agriculture to veterans returning to their farms after he, Gram, and my mother moved to New Ulm, but he never farmed in his adult life. I wonder how much the separation hurt. If your entire life is lived through the land, so that not only your food but your livelihood and your self-worth are tied to it, what happens when the roots are yanked out? How can you reconnect with what has been lost?

When the founding fathers established New Ulm, they built away from the river to minimize the danger from flooding.

The first big street was German Street. The next level up was Main Street, then Broadway, then Washington. That's where the wealthy new immigrants built their big homes. As time went by, there was a need for expansion, so they established Summit Avenue, which overlooked the city in all its grandeur.

My grandmother's voice booms in my ear, even from the distance of her letter. She doesn't hear well, so she speaks loudly. What I hold in my hand is the first—and probably only—time she has acknowledged my need for stories and written them down. She is my last living link to a lot of family history, so lately I have been trying to make her stories tangible. She always tells me that she values the letters we write her even more than phone calls, because she can reread them. It goes both ways.

There, a father and son, the Fritsches, practiced medicine. The father was mayor during World War I and he and the city were chastised for their pro-German activities, and he was eventually forced to resign. The son, Ted, became a prominent eye surgeon, and we became good friends with them, as well as with Wyn and Marty Forsberg. Dr. Ted had a large, beautiful Northern Colonial on the edge of the bluff on Summit Avenue and land on the other side of Summit. It was here, overlooking the Cottonwood River, that the Fritsches had this orchard of more than forty trees. It had been sorely neglected, unpruned, and allowed to deteriorate until the trees were quite unproductive.

Neglect—and the ensuing unproductivity—is an unforgivable sin to my grandmother.

Dr. Ted approached Wyn and your grandfather about whether the trees could be salvaged to produce again. Wyn and Kerm thought they could, so they—with Kerm doing most of the work—spent hours pruning. This was before the development of other apple varieties, so these were tall trees.

An old tale about pruning: Keep removing inner branches

until you can throw a cat straight up and it comes down to the ground without hitting a branch.

So my grandparents pruned; they picked; they pressed cider. Peeled, sliced, sugared, baked. Ate.

In "Wild Apples," Thoreau writes that there are some flavors that are not meant to be tasted indoors. Specifically, he means apples. My grandparents had nothing to do with wild apples, but to an extent, even cultivated apples are still an outdoor flavor. Apples, pumpkins, hayrides—they're all in the same family, Hallmark images aside. They cannot be adequately translated within walls. Thoreau believes that

> to appreciate the wild and sharp flavors of these October fruits, it is necessary that you be breathing the sharp October or November air. The out-door air and exercise which the walker gets gives a different tone to his palate, and he craves a fruit which the sedentary would call harsh and crabbed. They must be eaten in the fields, when your system is aglow with exercise, when the frosty weather nips your fingers, the wind rattles the boughs or rustles the few remaining leaves, and the jay is heard screaming around. What is sour in the house a bracing walk will make sweet. Some of these apples might be labelled, "To be eaten in the wind."

In October, we walk the dirt roads around Third Crow Wing, down along the lake paths, down the Heartland Trail close to my parents' house. All the fruits that sweetened the summer are long gone, and only a few remaining leaves are pinned to their branches. The wind—no longer soft enough to be called a breeze—is best described as invigorating. It gets the blood moving. It's a season of movement, after all. Minnesota in late fall sees a mass exodus of snowbirds, people who summer in Minnesota and winter in the South, and perhaps it's no accident that the best fruit that Minnesota has to offer is ready after they leave. Its summer fruits are nearly indistinguishable from any other place in the world—but Minnesota is an apple state at heart. Not many people are aware of this. It's not an apple state in the way that Washington is, but the University of Minnesota is well-known around the world for the quality of the apples it has developed over the last several decades. Their mission has been to develop hardy apples that grow in extreme conditions, the cold Minnesota winters and scorching Minnesota summers.

On the University of Minnesota's Apple website, the majority of its prizes are late-season apples. The state took its cues from northern Asia, since our climate is colder than most places that grow apples, and it was in Kazakhstan that the apple finds its parent soil. The university's program started in 1865 with 150 varieties, and new genes were added from New England apples, Midwest apples, and wild apples. Thoreau would have liked that. The website also reports:

> The record-breaking cold winter of 1917–1918 helped sort out the winners and the losers. Some progeny of "Malinda" genes, a New England apple, survived and led to the successful apples released in the 1920s, including "Haralson" and "Beacon." Some "Malinda" genes live on in varieties released decades later, including "Honeygold" and even "Honeycrisp."

The cold separated the winners and losers and I think Thoreau would have liked that too.

Michael Pollan, in *The Botany of Desire,* wonders about a different effect of natural selection: planting an apple seed is the most glorious kind of genetic experiment, since a tree that grows from an apple seed will only bear the faintest resemblance to its parent genetics. He writes, "Wherever the apple tree goes, its offspring propose so many different variations on what it means to be an apple—at least five per apple, several thousand per tree—that a couple of these novelties are almost bound to have whatever qualities it takes to prosper in the tree's adopted home." Later, he writes, "Like the settlers themselves, [the apple] had to forsake its former domestic life and return to the wild before it could be reborn as American . . . [and] in a remarkably short period of time, the New World had its own apples, adapted to the soil and climate and day length of North America, apples that were as distinct from the old European stock as the Americans themselves."

Several years ago now, Gram came from Minnesota to visit me in Ohio, where I was living. Eighty-two years old, five foot seven, slender, with eyes only a shade lighter blue than her daughter's, she tires easily, given her various health concerns, but she still has more intensity than anybody else I know. My grandfather had fallen and broken his pelvis a few weeks before and was recovering nicely in a nursing home under the watchful eyes of the nurses he likes to flirt with—and who like to flirt with him—so she didn't have to find anybody to take care of him. The apples at the orchard outside Toledo were ripe, so we went to pick some up. Johnny Appleseed was active in this area of the Northwest Territory, and according to Pollan, in order to receive a land grant in this area settlers were required to plant "fifty apple or pear trees" as a condition. Settlers were literally putting down roots—a different kind of roots from those who plant cereal crops.

We walk into the market area of MacQueen's Orchard, and Gram peruses the varieties offered, commenting on all of them. It's impossible for my grandmother not to voice an opinion if she has one, and she always has one. It would be irritating if she didn't know what she was talking about—but she always knows. And this is wonderfully comforting. *Have you tried Honeycrisps? The University of Minnesota came up with that one a few years ago*—1991, to be precise—*and at those orchards where you can pick your own, you can never pick Honeycrisps.* I nod, unable to get a word in. I learned that Honeycrisps had been designated the Minnesota State Apple in 2006, and once Honeycrisp trees were available at nurseries, they sold out almost immediately. *Jonathans are all-around good apples.* She frowns at the green Granny Smiths. *Granny Smiths are good in a pinch, but I don't use them anymore because they are too sour.* As if to prove that she is not utterly provincial, she notes that she prefers the New Zealand Braeburns, but there aren't any here.

There were a lot of the summer apples, which mature in August, in the Fritsches' orchard. One, I remember, was the Duchess. It was so juicy, made excellent pies, and our favorite, mushy applesauce. There were several kinds of crab that were early too—Whitney was one of them. They were an inch or so in diameter, great for eating. Those were what we used for apple pickles. They were cooked whole with sugar and spices and then canned. Sorry, I don't have the recipe. When served, you held them by the little spike handle and ate around the core. *It was okay to eat them like that in polite company.*

They farmed Greenings, which were similar to Granny Smiths. *Prairie Spy apples,* she said, *were beautiful, colorful, and very good eating. They made beautiful applesauce, and it looked so nice in those fruit jars in the basement cellar.* The Haralson, introduced in 1922, was the reigning king of Minnesota apples until it was deposed by the Honeycrisp. On the phone one night with my sister, I told her I was waiting for my baked apple to cool down enough so I could eat it. I told her it was a Honeycrisp, and before I could say they made the best baked apples I ever had, she rolled right over me with the sad observation, "Too bad it's not a Haralson."

Firesides were the best-tasting apple ever, Gram continued, *but it had to ripen fully on the tree or it tasted like a potato. They were no good for cooking or baking.* I remember Firesides from my childhood, vaguely, but I haven't tasted one in twenty years or more. *Red Delicious apples are no good for anything. They've been messed with so many times that there's no taste or texture there anymore.* There were two trees of Delicious in the Fritsches' orchard, gorgeous red, and Gram thought they tasted better than Washington's Delicious apples. These, she said, were Dr. Ted's special ones, the apples he gave as special gifts to his friends.

A side story about the Delicious. Since this orchard had become a backdrop for many new homes built by the 1950s elite residents of New Ulm, we knew they looked with envy on the orchard across the fence. One afternoon, I was up in the tree picking when the wife of the local shoe store owner came over with a pail and began picking apples. She didn't know I was there. "Did the Fritsches give you permission to pick those?" I asked.

Quite flustered, she said, "Well, no, but . . ."

I said, "If you'd like to purchase apples, you can do so at the shed. We aren't allowing others to pick."

She took her nearly empty pail and left and never bothered us again.

Pollan delights in the spectacular names of the apple varieties that he encounters, but as he laments the lost qualities of those apples, I mourn with him even as I am excited over the prospect of all of an apple's possibilities. How could anyone ever describe an apple as boring when some "tasted like bananas, others like pears. Spicy apples and sticky-sweet ones, apples sprightly as lemons and others rich as nuts." What a glorious orchard that would be.

Years later, I would call my mother from my local grocery store in Nebraska, thrilled that I found not only Haralsons for sale but also Firesides. It had been more time than I remembered since I had tasted either one.

"Make sure the Firesides aren't green," my mother said.

"I know," I said. "Or it tastes like a potato."

My mother laughed. "Your grandmother would be so proud you remembered."

I laughed too. "I was taught by the best," I said.

Here's what I want right now, as I'm surrounded by all of these Ohio apples at MacQueen's: I want to stand on the shore of Third Crow Wing Lake, on my grandparents' stretch of shoreline, take a bite of Minnesota, and let its juices drip off my chin and run down my arm. I want to, as one of Tim O'Brien's characters says in *The Things They Carried*, "eat this place." She is speaking of Vietnam. "I want to swallow the whole country—the dirt, the death—I just want to eat it and have it there inside me." I want to truly live off this land I still call home, though my address labels haven't carried that designation for years. I want to consume my home state as fuel, have it produce my energy, my red blood cells, everything that a human requires to function. I want Minnesota to become a part of my physical structure, to be more than a part of my emotion and history.

But for now, at MacQueen's Orchard, surrounded by my grandmother's voice, I merely want the apples any way I can get them. Samples of "fresh pressed apple cider" are available for ten cents. I get one for me and one for Gram, and she pronounces it "too zippy." We watch cider being made through a Plexiglas window and debate whether or not "fresh pressed cider" is grammatically correct.

The final "big deal" of the fall was the apple-squeezing party. The Fritsches invited us, of course, and a lot of their friends to the squeezing. We could bring our own apples if we wanted, and we used the bruised windfalls from the orchard that we wouldn't sell. First, the apples were washed in a clean stock tank and then put into a machine that chopped them into pieces. They were laid two inches deep on clean burlap that was about fifteen inches square. This was repeated until there were about eight to ten layers. Then a clamp was placed on top, and the hydraulic pressure forced the juice into a container. Then the remains were cleaned off and discarded, and the process was repeated many times. That juice was so sweet, all those different varieties of apples. We took it home in our own buckets, and I froze it in probably a dozen half-gallon milk cartons that I got from a local dairy.

When I lived in Washington State, some friends and I once took a road trip from Spokane to the wine country around Walla Walla. In one Washington winery, I learned the real meaning of "pretentious" from a vintner who believed we were in no way worthy of his wine. We sampled three syrahs—same grape, same winemaking process, same aging time, same barrels made of the same wood, but three different vineyards in the Walla Walla valley. Three different plots of land, three different soil compositions, three different rainfalls, and three different wines. You could taste the difference. When I buy apple juice in a store, and the label says it contains juice from apples from the United States, Brazil, or elsewhere, the lack of specificity bothers me. I want to know where these apples come from—and I want to know what kind they are.

Hard cider was the drink of choice in the days of the Colonies because the grapes that grew in New England were too bitter to make good wine—and, as Pollan writes, even the staunchest of Puritans could justify drinking hard cider while condemning the intoxication of wine. When water quality was dubious, drinking such things was the healthy alternative—and certainly tastier. In Ireland, I quickly became enamored of the various hard ciders available in the pubs, preferring them to the spreads of beer. According to the Bulmers website, my favorite cider, they use seventeen different apples with the most amazing names—Michelin, Dabinett, Yarlington Mill, Bulmer's Norman, Tremlett's Bitter, Breakwell Seedling, Taylor's, Harry Master's Jersey, Medaille d'Or, Reine des Pommes, Ashton Bitter, Bramley's, Grenadier, Brown Thorn, Brown Snout, Vilberies, and Improved Dove—and they make full use of the early, middle, and late apples. While commercially available American cider is delightful, there is something about Irish cider—and maybe it is the memory of the soil it grew in—that cannot be repeated.

Thoreau writes of cider apples, advocating to "let the frost come to freeze them first, solid as stones, and then the rain or a warm winter day to thaw them, and they will seem to have borrowed a flavor from the heaven through the medium of the air in which they hang." Ice wines are made this way, letting the grapes freeze on the vine, increasing the sugar content to such a level that you can only drink a very small amount of the wine before you're overwhelmed by the sweetness. I'm already over-whelmed, and I still want more. But Gram is here now, and she's teaching me about apples, and it's very good.

When we get home, Gram and I nap before attempting the pies. She brought me a pastry cloth from Minnesota, but she can't find it in her suitcase and concludes she must have left it at home. Irritated with herself, she puts the shortening in the fridge, then decides it won't cool quickly enough there, so she puts it in the freezer for a while.

Where's your rolling pin?

I point to the cupboard where I keep it. It's a solid cylinder of oak, without handles, and she looks at me with pity.

This really isn't a good kind of rolling pin. Get yourself a good one with handles—it will get your hands out of the way—and make sure it's not too skinny. Your sister has one of the skinny ones and it doesn't work very well either. She slides the rolling pin cover onto it.

First step: Measure the flour, salt, and baking powder. She hovers while I scoop the all-purpose white flour from the bag with the cup measure, tap the top with a knife to get an accurate measuring, then scrape the excess off with the knife.

You sure measure flour funny, she says.

I look at her. *This is the way you taught me to do it.*

She shakes her head.

Second step: Cut in the shortening. I obviously have improved my cutting technique from the last time, because she doesn't correct me. Cutting in the shortening is all about cutting it into small pieces, just like it sounds. It doesn't mean mixing things around—I learned that last time. Straight down, then scoop off the bottom and to the sides to make sure all the flour has come into contact with the shortening.

Parental cooking was out of necessity. In the early 1980s, my mother used to make a hotdish with elbow macaroni, ground beef, and tomatoes. In early 1984, our family came to call it Walter Mondale Hotdish after my father came home one night, looked at dinner, and wondered, "Where's the beef?" (a tagline Mondale used in his campaign, adopted from a Wendy's commercial). When served a similar dish at kindergarten, apparently I called it by that name, which prompted the cook to call my mother and tell her what her offspring had said. I don't remember much of cooking with my mother, the practical day-to-day cooking. Whatever cooking we did with Gram was dessert, in both the figurative and literal sense. Nobody could survive on pie, though I believe my father would have liked to try.

Third step: Add one tablespoon of vinegar to a half cup of cold water. The cold water is to help the shortening stay solid. I take the water out of the pitcher I keep in the fridge, and Gram looks at me with approval. Make wells with a spoon or spatula and pour the water into the wells. Chop with the spatula to incorporate. Do not stir.

After this step, all the cooking shows I have watched

say to let the dough rest for half an hour to let the glutens relax, whatever that means. Gram has never done this. And I guess that means I never will either.

Fourth step: Flour the pastry cloth and the rolling pin. Put half the dough on the pastry cloth. Press down with your hand so it is flatter. Smush the sides so that the edges aren't rough. Flip and repeat. Flip and repeat. It will save you headaches in the long run.

Fifth step: Roll out the dough. Start in the middle with the rolling pin and roll out, pressing firmly. Do not start on one edge and move across. Use as few strokes as possible to get the crust to the right thickness. Measure the crust with the pie tin to make sure the crust is large enough. If not, keep rolling. If you have breaks in your dough, or places where you have a fjord of emptiness where there should be crust, tear off a piece from a plentiful area and patch. I need to patch a lot.

Sixth step: Place the pie tin facedown on the dough and cut the dough about an inch beyond the tin. Allow for the sides of the tin. Remove excess dough. Roll the dough up on the pin and gently unroll the crust in the pie tin. Sprinkle some sugar and some flour in the bottom of the crust, especially if you are making a fruit pie. This will help the crust become stiffer on the bottom so the fruit doesn't soak through.

This first pie of ours will be Minnesota blueberry, from a plastic container of blueberries she brought in her suitcase. These aren't wild berries from their secret picking ground somewhere deep in the Badoura State Forest— owing to their age, it has been many years since she and Grandpa have been physically able to pick there. When my sisters and I were little, we always had pies and syrups made of wild blueberries, a cousin to Thoreau's wild apples, except that wild blueberries are meant to be eaten when the sun warms the shallow waters of Third Crow Wing Lake to the temperature of bathwater. Gram's blueberries have thawed, and we have sugared them, added some flour, and decided they need a kick of salt and lemon juice. Gram plucks one out with her fingers to test. Good! We pile the blueberries into the pie tin, add some butter so things don't burn, then roll out and place the top crust. I tuck the edge of the top crust under the bottom crust and pinch with my fingers to seal. I press the tines of a fork into the edge of the crust to ensure a seal and to decorate. I take a knife and poke a K and a P into the crust to ventilate. Karen. Phyllis.

We make a full-size apple pie the same way, then two small ones in tins I bought a year ago. While I manipulate the piecrust, Gram peels the apples. She approves of my peeler, thank goodness, but she's not far enough away to miss when I screw up rolling out the dough. She cuts up the apples, and I pour a cup of sugar and a bit of flour over them and mix them up. I pick one of the sugar-covered apple pieces and pop it into my mouth.

Gram looks at me. *I never thought you kids liked that,* she says.

What? I ask.

Sugar-covered apples, she says.

I smirk. *You cover anything in that much sugar and we'll eat it.*

She smiles, snitches an apple for herself. Maybe because a pie is designed to be cut into six or eight pieces and shared, the inheritance of the apples is more than the roots that define its origins.

Later, I will fill a bowl on my kitchen table with Honeycrisps, this apple that was literally born in Minnesota soil. I have bought Honeycrisps that were grown in Ohio soil, as well as some from Washington State and elsewhere. Does it matter where their descendant seedlings are grown? Will they always retain some genetic remembering of the place they began? I hope so. I hope that even if I bite into a Honeycrisp from Ohio—or some other unknown place—that I will be able to taste Minnesota and follow the apple's roots back to the soil that formed my bones.

In *Staying Put,* Scott Russell Sanders writes, "If you are not yourself *placed,* then you wander the world like a sightseer, a collector of sensations, with no gauge for measuring what you see. Local knowledge is the grounding for global knowledge." Since we ship our produce in from around the country and around the world, sometimes we don't know what place we're eating, and our brains can't process the information. We can't tell how the soil affected the flavor of the grape, the tomato, the potato, the pomegranate. But, even so, does some part of us still know? As Pollan traces the life paths of the apple, looking for the desire for sweetness it represented before that desire was polluted with sugar, I wonder if the sweetness of apples—of whatever variety—must now come from what happens after the apple has been picked, when peeler meets fruit, when dough is rolled out and Gram corrects my mistakes. Is this the pruning necessary to a life, the necessary transplanting and grafting to make sure a plant takes? I like the idea of my life as a graft of my previous generations, not an apple seed planted in the ground to be its own genetic experiment, remembering little of the genes that brought me to this place at this time.

And so here we are, standing in my Ohio kitchen, baking pies, transplanting a life, and hoping the roots will take.

Water and What It Knows

I. Sjöberg
sjö, lake; *berg,* mountain (Swedish)

Most of the surnames of my Swedish ancestors indicate that someone put some stock into where they came from. Their name was not only where they lived, but it became who they were. That is a very solid, comforting thought. Identity as tangible, your name and your history literally a place to return to.

Thorsander: *Thor,* Ostra Torsas (a region in Sweden); *ander,* where they came from. Holm: *holm,* small island. Dahlberg: *dahl,* valley; *berg,* mountain. And Sjöberg, eventually anglicized to Shoberg.

Sjöberg is pronounced *wheh-berg.* (Shoberg is much easier for the average American to say, probably why they changed the pronunciation and spelling.) The first syllable is little more than a puff of air, hardly a vocal sound at all. *Wheh.* As if you're blowing out a candle, gently, so that you don't get wax all over everything. Along Highway 10 in Lake Park, Minnesota, there is a gorgeous church along the road called Eksjö, a bit of Swede in the vastly Norwegian prairie landscape. *Ek,* oak; *sjö,* lake. Lake Park. *Ek-wheh.* But the locals say *ek-sho.* My grandmother reports that some of the old-timers in Shafer, one of the many small, Swedish towns in the very Swedish Chisago County of east-central Minnesota, use the Swedish pronunciation and call the town *whey-fer.* In Chisago County, you can still hear Swedish spoken on the street. It is not as prevalent as it once was, but the language is still important here.

There were probably mountains where the Sjöbergs came from in Sweden, but there are none in Minnesota, in Chisago County, where the people pronounced the name right. There are no mountains, but there are lakes. The land, bearing their names, felt good and right beneath their plows, between their fingers. They were used to harsh climates, but Minnesota was a different breed of place. *Sjöberg* no longer accurately reflected where they were from. The Sjöbergs are no longer of the lake and the mountain. Who are they now?

II. Minnesota

mine, water; *sota,* somewhat clouded (Dakota)

There's good reason why Minnesotans dry up when separated from the water of their home state. Ecology and psychology are at work here, a chemistry of place, but a linguistic element is also at play. Our connection to water starts in the most basic places, and it's most obvious in the names we chose to identify those places, such as our state name. Near the Twin Cities of Minneapolis and St. Paul, you'll find a suburb named Minnetonka (big water) and a waterfall named Minnehaha, meaning falling water, not laughing water. Half of the Twin Cities, Minneap-

olis, is a lovely linguistic hybrid of Ojibwe and Greek—
minne means water, and *polis* means city—city of water. Up
north, Camp Minne-Wa-Kan, where I worked during college, translates to *spirited water.* But because that did not
seem appropriate for a Bible camp, we chose to translate
the name as *spirit over the water.*

For Minnesotans, water is, at its root, a language.
Water is the way by which we can understand ourselves,
each other, and the surrounding world. It is how we communicate. Water is how we connect with the land under
our feet, the land under our plows and our combines. It
is the way we know where we are geographically, who we
are personally, and who we are as a community. Humanity may be able to connect more clearly with the more
physically consistent land, but Minnesotans, residents of
the Land of 10,000 Lakes, must also reconcile their relationship to water because the native ground of a Minnesotan is water, not land. Water is what Minnesotans do
for fun; it is what we build dikes and levies to protect
against. We worry about our land, whether sand or clay,
because of how the water works on it. Hubbard County
never floods; the Red River Valley does so nearly every
time it rains more than an inch or two.

We want to be surrounded by all the forms water can
take because humanity is not predictable and constant.
We want the ice, we want the snow, we want the rain, the
hail, the flood—even when the presence of water is destructive, it still reminds us that water is a give and take,
and we can't always have it good. We want the humility
that water brings. It reminds us that things can always be
worse. The water gets into a Minnesotan's personality
permanently. And the path to that ecological reconcilia-
tion is linguistic.

III. Winter

In high school, I learned that water is one of very few substances that expand when frozen. Because frozen water is less dense than liquid water, it freezes from the top down, making life possible in the lakes even when the air temperature is well below zero. Water is sticky, which enables its surface tension to support floating objects. Water's unusual physical properties correspond to the weather, where water presents another paradox: forty-below winter temperatures are not exactly canceled out by hundred-degree summer days when the air is liquid with humidity, sending the heat index further up into the triple digits, humidity that feels like a sticky second skin. But the best relief from such humidity is to jump in the nearest lake, submerge oneself completely in the water, surrender to the inevitability of water in one form or another.

Minnesota smiles at knowing that both *water* and *winter* share the same word root. She laughs at her people, who find no irony in fishing on the surface of the water in summer as well as in winter. This spectrum of temperatures finds particular irony in the winter. Sometimes it is just too cold to snow, or at least in the sense we consider *cold* and *snow*. When I was little, I couldn't understand this, but cold air cannot hold water, and if there is no water, there is no snow. Meteorologists also point out that because Antarctica is so cold, the snowfall in certain areas is so minimal that it is actually classified as desert. Minus ten degrees is about the cutoff point for snow. Fred W. Decker of the Oregon Climate Service at Oregon State University explains on ScientificAmerican.com:

> At higher, but still subfreezing, temperatures, ice crystals hook onto each other to create snowflakes.

In extreme cold, the ice crystals remain independent. There actually is no such thing as too low a temperature for some sort of ice crystal to form and for such crystals to settle out and land on the surface. Such a deposit of ice needles is not usually considered "snow," however; in the Arctic, for instance, we might refer instead to an ice fog.

So, technically, snow is always possible, but not in the form of falling snow that we normally think of. The same type of thinking applies to blizzards. In some places in Minnesota "blizzard" refers to large quantities of falling snow and enough wind to make conditions dangerous, but in the prairies, we are more likely to have ground blizzards, where snow on the ground is driven into the air and drifted across roads by strong winds. Once, I got caught in a ground blizzard driving back to Fargo from Minneapolis, and the interstate turned into the most terrifying driving experience I can remember. I could not see the taillights of the car in front of me and had only the smallest sense of where the road actually was.

At minus forty degrees, Celsius and Fahrenheit are the same temperature.

Much fun can be had when the temperature gets down that low. Below minus ten it rarely snows, but once the thermometer hits minus forty, if you toss a cup of boiling water into the air, the water will vaporize before it hits the ground. It's pretty amazing to fling that water into the air and watch it poof into a cloud for a moment, then disappear in the next instant. My senior year of high school, the governor canceled school across the state twice because the air temperatures—not the windchill—were supposed to go down to minus sixty degrees Fahrenheit. The first time it did; the second was only minus forty. The novelty of the boiling water was so much fun that my mother ended up standing in the kitchen with her hands on her hips, laughing, giving my father dirty looks for starting the whole thing and winding up my two sisters and me before bed. My father just looked back at her and grinned.

For Minnesotans, more than a psychological connection exists between us and snow. Snow is necessary, on many different levels. Of course, it's fun. There are snowmen to be rolled, snowball fights to be had, walks in a winter wonderland that end with hot chocolate. In old photo albums, I have found pictures of me at age three or four, bundled up in my snowsuit, and the snowbanks along the sidewalk are taller than I am. My sisters and I used to build elaborate forts, not only in our yard where Dad had pushed all the snow from our driveway but also across the street in the Catholic church's parking lot, where all that snow had been pushed into an immense pile. We were the only kids in the vicinity, so it was ours for the taking. We built tunnels and stockpiled icicle weapons and snowballs against intruders, but the three of us never had the war we prepared for because we didn't want to destroy our masterpiece forts. But there's more to snow than fun.

On a purely practical level, if the ground freezes and not enough snow has fallen to provide insulation, pipes will freeze and burst. Snow has immense insulating properties, and I know some scientific studies have compared it to standard insulation. I don't understand the jargon, but I know we need snow—or in its absence, straw—to keep my grandparents' drain field and pipes from freezing. I remember in college a couple of friends spending some time at Wolf Ridge on the North Shore, overlooking Lake Superior, and when they returned, they told me they had spent the night in a snow cave. They said that if you have a small heat source, like a candle or even just body heat, you can be fairly comfortable. Not only that, if you're caught outside in a blizzard, your chances of surviving are much greater if you make yourself a snow cave, because the temperature inside a snow cave never goes below freezing. I have never put this to the test.

On an economic level, if there isn't enough snow, tourists don't come to Lakes Country. They need snow and cold to ice fish, to snowmobile, to cross-country ski, to fish at the Eelpout Festival in Walker. I gave up fishing before I hit double digits; I have never been snowmobiling. I used to enjoy cross-country skiing when I was younger, but I always managed to fall and wrench joints when I tried to stand after falling. Downhill skiing is a sort of wonder in Minnesota, since we don't have mountains— not that I am brave enough to literally risk life and limb for that sort of fun. But there are those who do.

On a recreational level, the more snow the better— for tourists and for us too. Snowballs. Snowmen. Snow angels. Until my parents moved from Nevis, my youngest sister, who had not yet graduated from high school, liked to make snow angels on top of their garage roof. The colder the temperature, the more mighty I feel. It is a pride thing—I especially liked to shock our California relatives with our tales of below-zero temperatures. They have never come to Minnesota to visit us, in any season, seemingly convinced that Minnesota is cold all year long. I remember when we went out to California for Christmas once, and Grandmother came outside to greet us, wrapped in her long wool coat, gloves, and scarf.

We laughed. We were in our short sleeves. It was fifty degrees.

The bottom line is that Minnesota needs snow, even if we can't articulate it clearly. If we don't have snow, parts of us begin to die.

IV. Language of Light

When I moved to Spokane, my mother's cousin warned me that while Minnesota winter skies are most often blue, the customary gray skies over eastern Washington cause seasonal affective disorder in many people. I didn't believe him right away, but so many days would pass without sun that I would lose track of when I last needed my sunglasses. Something amazing inhabits this paradox so common to Minnesota and the Midwest: blue skies and sunshine and very, very cold temperatures.

What I love most about blue skies and cold temperatures has everything to do with breathing. How can people breathe with so much cloud cover? There's something elemental in the sharpness of the inhale, feeling the molecules of cold shoot to your fingertips down every inch of your veins. It hurts to breathe deeply, but you do it anyway because you have to. Stand up straight. Breathe in slowly, but fill yourself. Pretend you are a singer. Don't just fill up your lungs, but your abdomen as well. None of these short, shallow inhales that allow your body heat to thaw the air before it hits your lungs. Fill yourself until your toes and fingers begin to swell with air. Then you will know what it is like to be truly alive.

Interestingly enough, the word *cloud* is a lovely paradox: the word in Middle English means a *hill,* but in Old English, it translates not only to *hill* but also to *rock.* Not exactly *water.* The assumption is that "cloud" means *to obscure.* But this etymology is a bit troubling, especially for a Minnesotan, whose name means *somewhat-clouded water.* How can a thing that is made up of water come from a word that is the exact opposite of water? We believe that water and land cannot peacefully coexist. One will always dominate. But here there is one word for two combative elements. How can that be? Can we hold several mutually exclusive elements inside ourselves without the juxtaposition tearing us apart?

If cloud cover blocked Minnesota winter skies, then the difference between winter light and summer light would be less obvious. This is likely due to the reflective qualities of snow and ice, but the difference in the light can't be explained by that alone. Light certainly does not reflect off grass the way it does off snow. In the winter, you can wake up in the middle of the night and find your bedroom is light enough to navigate without turning on a lamp, or you can look out the window and see what mariners called "whiskers 'round the moon," ice crystals around the moon. Of course, this was a bad omen if you were on the water at the time; crew members saw this phenomenon the night the *Titanic* sank. Or you might see a spread of stars so sharp that they nearly hurt, as if you could feel the prickles on your skin. With cloud cover, sun dogs would not be visible.

Aurora borealis, northern dawn (Latin). I would like to describe them as writhing ribbons of color or something equally fanciful, but the northern lights are not always ribbons. There are several different forms, from rays to curtains. The most brilliant I ever saw in the summer were aqua blue, above Lake Andrusia in northern Minnesota. In the winter, mint-green lights were almost blinding. It has been many years since I have seen the northern lights, long enough that when I remember them, I am not sure my memories are accurate. I remember a photograph I saw during the 1997 spring flood of the Red River: a field covered in water, a blurred barn in the background, and brilliant northern lights, vibrant blues and greens, reflected in the floodwaters.

Sun dogs are a welcome sight, those rainbow-colored bookends of the sun. "Parhelion" is the scientific term—from the Greek *para,* beside, and *helios,* sun—a word that tastes as good as it sounds. Sun dogs are the result of the sun's rays being bent through ice crystals, which act as prisms. Sun and ice, light and warmth. Opposites can certainly exist in the same sphere. If they didn't, we wouldn't have rainbows in the winter.

V. Lake of the Woods
Lac du Bois (French)

Lake of the Woods Bible Camp, known affectionately by its acronym LOWBC, pronounced *low-beck,* sister camp to Minne-Wa-Kan, sits on the Rainy River in the far north of Minnesota; on the other side of the river is Canada. Every Wednesday during the four summers I worked there during college, we took the kids for an afternoon to Zippel Bay State Park, which is on Lake of the Woods. My first time there, I didn't understand the empty watercoolers we packed into the van. I was told we would fill them at the spring, but I didn't understand what that meant either.

The spring wasn't too far from the swimming beach, and when my fellow staff members emptied their water bottles and filled them with spring water, I did the same. Now I understood. The water at LOWBC is not known for its purity. The spring water, however, was everything water should be. Cool, clear, sweet. After the day was over, we filled the coolers with water, took them back to camp, and hid them in the kitchen. The campers had to drink the camp water, and we didn't tell them our bottles held good water. The spring water became one of the perks of working at LOWBC. It was a place where we consumed the water of the spring even as we were consumed by the power of the lake itself.

The language to the Lake of the Woods is primal, a language without words. This was a place where the lake is so large that on the right day, at the right time of day, with the right slant of light, the lake is exactly the same color as the horizon, making the water and the sky one entity. Many people feel a calling when they are near the ocean, even if they have no desire to swim in it. Water is an exercise in humility. I am powerless, incapable of asserting myself if the water decides it wants to keep me. And maybe Minnesotans fear captivity as well, given what we have constructed to escape our dwellings during all four seasons.

Water is wild and will remain wild, in fluid conversation with the sky above. They are not as separate as we sometimes like to make them.

VI. River People

My college years were spent on a prairie in western Minnesota. I couldn't understand the language of the prairie; I couldn't understand the flatness of the land, the immensity of the sky, the lack of water. To be fair, I didn't really try. But in the intervening years, on the Great Plains of Nebraska and then back to the Red River Valley, I came to understand the prairie in a way I couldn't when I was eighteen. During those college years, I spent my time by the Red River and comforted myself with the knowledge that before long I would be back in Lakes Country. If I were to give a translation to the prairie, it would be the opposite of Minnesota. Sometimes in opposites we find the truest definitions.

The language of the eastern Montana prairie—and the other prairies I am familiar with—is not water but sky. My first real exposure to this came in August 1998, when I spent an afternoon on the Missouri River. My middle sister moved to Missoula, to the valley surrounded by the Bitteroot Mountains, for a few years, just for the experience of choosing to be somewhere else, and then she chose to come back to Minnesota. If she were to actually come from this place, if this place were to become part of who she is, not just her place of residence, I would call her a Dahlberg. Valley-mountain. We were Dahlbergs once upon a generation.

The Big Muddy offered up some contrasts I didn't expect. I wanted the water to be a constant, so that I could feel more comfortable being near it, but it wasn't. That was strange, and I tried to figure out why. Eventually, a possible answer came in the difference between river people and lake people. Lake people, like those of Lakes Country in Minnesota, don't seek anything beyond the shore. Those who settled Minnesota and dug themselves into the soil had no reason to look beyond. They had found what they needed. River people are always looking for more. Find yourself standing on the shore of a river like the Mississippi or the Missouri, and you will find yourself compelled to walk it. You may not know where you are going or why your legs don't obey your mind, but you will keep walking. You will keep wondering about where you'll end up. If you walk upriver along the Mississippi long enough, you will find its beginning, at Itasca, thirty miles from where I grew up. If you walk the other way, you will find yourself in New Orleans. Along the way, you will find another river. And another one. A lake is self-contained, complete. There is no need to wander. Everything you need is right there. In *Staying Put,* Scott Russell Sanders writes, "Riverness—the appeal of a river, the way it speaks to us—has to do with our craving for a sense of direction within the seeming randomness of the world. Narrative offers us the same pleasure, a shape and direction imposed on time. And so we tell stories and listen to them as we listen to the coursing of the water." But water is water and you take what you can get when nothing else is available.

I was nineteen years old. I had just finished my first year of college and was accompanying the youth group on a weeklong mission trip to Montana. My role was incredibly awkward—I wasn't one of the youth anymore, but I wasn't an adult either. On Tuesday, we planned to spend the afternoon canoeing on the Missouri River. I had been drafted—as a semiadult, a role I had no language for—into a canoe that held two rowdy fifteen-year-old boys. It would be an interesting afternoon.

The summer-warmed water was a benefit, since the boys in my canoe wanted to be in front and splashed anyone who came near. Not having a paddle of my own, I assisted with my hands, which was not particularly effective. Our lead remained unchallenged for several miles, but when the boys became bored with splashing, they wanted to tip anyone who came close.

And we did.

We called ourselves the Missouri River Bandits, and we made it our mission to tip every canoe, and we did, except for the "safe canoe." It was great fun. At the sandbars, the lot of us—fifteen or so—covered ourselves in mud, tossed mud, and explored the mud. Covered in mud myself, I stood at the edge of the sandbars in ankle-deep water, noticing the unusual sensation of the world dissolving under my bare feet. Hours later, I could still feel the sand flowing away. As I walked across it, the sand was firmly packed, but something in the current of the river and the shallows shifted the sand whenever I stopped and stood. It almost tickled. For a lake person who wants to stay put, it was unnerving. The river itself was literally compelling my movement.

Trevor and Brian had something to do with compelling my movement as well. They covertly got my attention, and the three of us jumped in our canoe and headed downstream before anyone noticed that we had all the paddles.

VII. *the lake into which the river pitches and ceases to flow* (Ojibwe)

Lake Belle Taine, formerly known as Elbow Lake, remembers little of its original Ojibwe name except the translation. Nobody knows where "Belle Taine" came from either, but that's a different story. All that remains is a lake, one of seventeen in the Mantrap Chain carved up by glaciers aeons ago, into which water flows but from which there is no outlet. Belle Taine is one of ninety lakes in a ten-mile radius at the heart of Lakes Country in north-central Minnesota. My hometown is built on its shores; my childhood home is three blocks from the beach.

The beach was such a commonplace memory in my childhood that what I remember most comes out of the unusual moments: biking to and from Dorset on the Heartland Trail, five miles away, and sometimes our parents would let us swim in our clothes. When it was really hot—we did not have air conditioning—our parents would take us down to the beach before bed and let us swim. We would bring our dog, our beautiful beagle-springer mix, Katy, who absolutely loved water and unerringly found the dead fish every time we visited our grandparents' lake. How rare it was that our parents went in the water with us. I remember how much I took that water for granted, how easy it was to walk the three blocks in bare feet, how much extra effort it must have been for everyone else to pack up their cars and drive there.

Until only a few years ago, the lake level wasn't a problem, as drought and the sugar sand geology kept Belle Taine at a manageable level. When I was younger, spending all my summer free time at the beach, I used to measure the lake level by the square of concrete on which the lifeguard's chair was perched. I remember that at the time we moved to Nevis, the water lapped at the base of the concrete, but in the following years, dry yards separated the red chair and the lip of the lake. Then in June 2001, the lake hit its highest level in recorded history, nearly five feet higher than average.

Homes built before the one-hundred-feet-from-the-lake requirement were in trouble. The sandbagging against floodwaters so common in the Red River Valley to the west now became a common sight around Belle Taine residences. The public beach was suffering from so much erosion that a retaining wall was built to hold in the hill. Lawns turned into swamps, perfect mosquito breeding grounds.

Eventually, the city lost its public landing, the only public landing on Belle Taine. The city council decided that if the landing remained impassable, the tourists would take their boats and money and go elsewhere, so the council dumped truckloads of sand so that vacationers and locals would be able to use the landing. They built a retaining wall at the beach—which wasn't really a beach anymore, no longer a place to build sand castles.

At the time and in the immediate years after, the county did little more than fight over how to resolve this problem. They brought in the DNR to assess options, but nothing happened. These days, more than ten years later, the lake level has returned to normal, but the culture of the area has changed: resorts sold off their cabins individually, changing how tourists experience the water, and lake property values have skyrocketed. I wonder how the ecological balances the psychological. How is our language complicated when water is stilled against its will? When the water is clouded by something other than sky? What happens to our language when streams are dammed? When I walk along the Columbia River in Washington, or other Pacific Northwest rivers, stand at the Grand Coulee Dam—what is the real effect of this? Do we destroy or just complicate our ability to understand the world around us?

VIII. Translating a Rant of Rain and Wind

The winter rains were a continual presence in Ireland for most of my six months there. As I recall, it was raining when I arrived. Except for the expected green of the grass, everything else was gray: the sky, the Atlantic, the rain, the stones. Minnesota rain is not like Irish rain. Irish rain is influenced by proximity to the ocean, which produces thick mists and light patters that don't really require a raincoat, and Minnesota rains are the result of clashing fronts of hot and cold air masses. I much prefer storms to gentle downpours or mists, another reason I love Minnesota, the northern portion of Tornado Alley, where the summer rains are much like my bad moods—vicious but never lasting very long. The storms bring bruising rain, hail that dents cars and crops, winds that lay waste to all obstacles, and then an hour later, it's calm, and there's a blue sky in its wake.

Perhaps a Minnesotan's relationship with water stems from the realization that water is both life-giving and life-taking. It is constructive and destructive. The residents of the Red River Valley between Minnesota and North Dakota know this well: they have tried to control the Red for years. Water is humbling; there is nothing we can do to beat it. We should know that by now, but we still fight it. We complain when there isn't enough water, and we complain when there is too much.

But sometimes we just play with it. Sometimes we just have to.

Minnesota is full of Scandinavian Protestants, people stereotyped as stoic and serious. The stereotype isn't all that far off. Minnesotans are, psychologically, middle-ground people. Despite Nebraska's new slogan of Nebraska Nice, we are the original Nice, and we are Nice enough to let Nebraska claim the term if it means that much to them. The water, extreme in both summer and winter, rarely finds this middle, so something has to. If anything, Minnesotans err on the side of serious. But it's not good to keep emotions bottled up, so maybe summer thunderstorms are the weather equivalent of Minnesotans losing their temper, yelling at the top of their lungs. My family still tells the story of the thunderstorm we went through in our pop-up camper in Glendive, Montana, the thunderstorm that hit when we were at Mount Vernon, Virginia.

One college summer day, while I was working at camp, the anticipation of the storm rippled along my skin like a promise. The air was heavy, still. I could very nearly taste the tension in the air, and it made me grin like a fool. I forget how many storm systems they say hit us that July day, but it thundered and tossed lightning all day, the clouds dropping about eight inches of rain in twelve hours. If it had been any other place, the damage from flooding would have been incredible, but we weren't in danger, because the Rainy emptied into the Lake of the Woods, which was large enough to handle the volume. We couldn't see the Rainy River in the darkness, but we could hear it, and the sound was as close to a growl as I have ever heard from water. When the storm had passed, the play started; various staff members were tossed into the mud and then dumped into the showers fully clothed. Usually this was the newbie staff initiation, but if we were short of new people, anybody was fair game. We were drunk on rain, high on thunder, buzzed on lightning.

What is the language of a thunderstorm? What happens within a Minnesota thunderstorm that we can't get elsewhere? Sometimes, it's just a purity of emotion made tangible by the weather. A thunderstorm may be what we are afraid to say. A thunderstorm may be a release from the constraints of Minnesota culture, which, at times, can feel restrictive. We could yell and scream and let loose all the messy emotions inside us and have it drowned out by the noise of the storm. There's a privacy there. A thunderstorm may give permission to say what I want, act how I want. It would be too exhausting to act that way all the time, but it is fun—and perhaps healthy—to act without caution once in a while.

During that storm, as well as many others that that summer, Carrie and I—the leadership staff—sat on the steps outside the dining hall, with the campers tucked safely downstairs with the counselors. We were twenty-two and invincible. We noted the difference in thunder as we sat there: there were rumbles that sounded like marbles on a hardwood floor, bass drum booms, and cracks that sounded like the sky was being cracked like an egg. With the phone in hand, the National Weather Service on speed dial, we watched the clouds rotate, rating the thunder on a scale of 1 to 10, often heckling, "Come on, God, just one funnel cloud—is that too much to ask?" We didn't actually want a tornado. We had seen the ravages they left behind. But we wanted to see, really *see,* the power held in that water and those clouds. We wanted to be surrounded, truly surrounded, by what made us wholly Minnesotan.

IX. The Pirate Ship

A blue heron named Freddy used to sit on the dock at the Cabin. We never knew if it was the same heron year after year, but it was always named Freddy. For all the loons we saw on that lake, we never named any of them. I have chilly memories of my sisters and I helping the adults put in the dock every spring, splashing a spring shower on those who worked in olive-green hip boots and long-sleeved wool shirts. It always seemed to be a frigid day. We jumped off the dock in the summer, but we were forbidden to go past the end of the dock until our ages reached double digits. We rowed black inner tubes the short distance from the dock to the birch trees leaning over the lake, their root systems dislodged by ice against the shore and the erosion of the sand. Eventually, the trees fell into the water, but this particular tree didn't until long after we were too big to need it as a pirate ship anymore. I remember standing with my sisters on that dock, rare quiet moments, fishing with just a stick and string, watching the sunnies in the shallow water. We never figured out why they could never be caught.

The River—1997

G round yourself.

    This is the southernmost part of Glacial Lake Agassiz that once covered parts of Saskatchewan, Manitoba, Ontario, North Dakota, and Minnesota during the last ice age. The lake itself was never static in size, changing as the glaciers advanced and retreated in Canada, but at its largest point, the lake may have covered as many as a quarter-million square miles. When it disappeared, about 7,500 years ago, it left behind several large lakes, including Lake Winnipeg, Lake of the Woods, Rainy Lake, and Red Lake. The rest of what remained was flat, thick-clay land. The land was not devastated, exactly, but because it had been underwater for so long, the aftermath of that long immersion would affect those who would call this place home.

    Narrow your focus down to a single thread, one river flowing northward from the confluence of the Bois du Sioux and Ottertail Rivers near Breckenridge in western Minnesota. The Red River of the North, the border between North Dakota and Minnesota, is born here. The

Red eventually empties into Lake Winnipeg in Ontario. Many North Dakota and Minnesota towns are sister cities, separated only by the river: Fargo, North Dakota, and Moorhead, Minnesota; Grand Forks, North Dakota, and East Grand Forks, Minnesota. We do not call them "twins" because that would cause confusion with the Twin Cities of Minneapolis and St. Paul, partly separated by the Mississippi. Most of the surrounding areas remain rural because the Red River Valley is some of the best farmland in the world. The early settlers had no idea why. They just knew that the land was so flat that if their dog ran away, they could watch him go for three days.

The glaciers of this area also carved up the Canadian Shield to the north, some of the oldest exposed rock in the world. The irony, according to Donald P. Schwert of North Dakota State University, is that "the Red River Valley of North Dakota/Minnesota is the youngest major land surface in the contiguous United States. . . . Therefore, whereas most river systems in the United States date in ages in the millions or even tens of millions of years, the present course of the Red River of the North is only a few thousands of years old." Old, young. Dry, wet. Land, water. Irony and contradiction have been a part of this place since the beginning.

Those who chose to hunt the animals on the prairie found an abundance. Those northern Europeans who took advantage of the Homestead Acts and the Dawes Act and saw empty land there for the taking, just waiting to be turned into something useful, learned that the soil, thick clay left from the silt of the lake bed, was perfect for crops once they rid themselves of the tall grasses that served no purpose they could see. It was difficult work to get the land tilled, but the results were worth it. But because the soil is largely clay, which does not drain, and because the Red is far too young to have carved its own floodplain, the entire valley is at risk when the Red spills its banks, which it does on a regular basis. Even a few inches of rain causes the Red to rise, and it takes several weeks before the river returns to its normal levels. Once the river overflows its boundaries, there's no place for the water to go but out. It's like watching an ice cube melt on a flat table.

The settlers of the Red River Valley may not have known that the soil caked into the cleats of their boots was once under a great deal of water ten thousand years ago, but the Red flooded nearly every year. They didn't like it, they tried to protect themselves and their property as best they could, but when the Red chose to flood, the water ceased to become a passive entity and took on a force nobody could control. This flabbergasted people who were used to believing that anything could be achieved with hard work, a strong back, and a little elbow grease. This culture had grown out of their ethnicity, their religion, and their landscape.

Starting in the late nineteenth century, these floods were recorded. The worst before 1997 was in 1897, when an estimated 85,000 cubic feet per second of water was measured at Grand Forks, North Dakota. Designations of floods were taken seriously by people who had had no previous reason to care. Ten-year floods were floods of a severity that could be expected every ten years. Since records were started in 1880, eleven ten-year floods have been recorded. This includes floods that passed the fifty-year flood mark. Of these there are four, between 1880 and 2000. The 1979 flood, which measured 82,000 cubic feet per second of water in Grand Forks, was, for many, the flood to end all floods because most didn't remember the 1897 flood. But in 1997, the Red River Valley saw its first one-hundred-year flood. Some called it a five-hundred-year flood. The flood of the millennium. Discharge at Grand Forks was measured at 136,000 cubic feet per second.

Pause here. Wrap your brain around those numbers again. Think of an ice cube melting on a flat table. A really big ice cube.

April 1997. I am eighteen years old, a senior in a high school one hundred miles to the west of Fargo–Moorhead. I have not yet broken out of the self-centered world that is high school. My concept of news and current events happens only in hindsight. It is winter in Minnesota. It snows. It's cold. This is nothing new. But those who are paying attention to such things know something is brewing and it will not be good.

The winter of 1996–97 was especially cruel in a place not easily surprised by winter weather. My parents' thermometer only measured to forty below, and several times the digital readout read *error* in the morning. I had three pet rabbits outside under the pine tree; I brought them inside when the temperatures reached such dangerous levels. The governor canceled school twice across the state because of dangerously cold temperatures, which got down to minus sixty. This was the air temperature, without taking into account the windchill factor. We were delighted, because when the governor cancels school, we don't have to make it up. This was my focus during these months, the antics of my pets, and I had no real capacity to care about anything outside my immediate world.

I might have noted the trivia that propane stops vaporizing at minus forty, but it wasn't something I really needed to know.

The threat of spring flooding started the fall before because of heavy precipitation in October and November, four inches above normal in many places. Over the winter months, many places received two or three times their average snowfall. Fargo–Moorhead, for example, received 117 inches of snow, compared to their average of 39 inches. We knew by January that the flood would be bad, so we started preparing, but we had no idea how bad it would be. When things started to melt in late March, people in the area started sandbagging. The river was rising, and the National Weather Service predicted a thirty-nine-foot crest of the river in Fargo–Moorhead and a forty-nine-foot crest in Grand Forks–East Grand Forks. Flood stage for Fargo–Moorhead is seventeen feet; for Grand Forks and East Grand Forks, it is twenty-six feet.

Sandbags were piled around homes to keep out the floodwaters, with sump pumps spewing the seepage back out. These fortifications took on the appearance of a war zone. Panic set in after Blizzard Hannah—they were named—settled over the valley from April 4 through 6. She brought sixty-mile-per-hour winds, twenty inches of snow, and then ice. Hannah didn't cause the river to stop rising; she added more to it, and nobody could be out there to stop it. We might have been able to beat the river if not for Hannah, but we'll never know.

After Hannah hit, Nevis High loaded up two buses full of students to sandbag in Fargo–Moorhead. When we got there, we sandbagged for a few hours, lining up in an assembly line to transfer fifty-pound bags of sand to the front lines. We didn't do as much work as we would have liked, as much as we were prepared to do. Fargo had put out a call for forty thousand volunteers to help on this day, and over a hundred thousand showed up. I recall that it was sunny but very cold. It was hard to keep hold of the sandbags. It's difficult, heavy work, especially with frozen fingers. And trying to handle fifty-pound sandbags when you're laughing like loons is even harder. We did have fun, as high school kids released from classes do.

Snapshots of memories remain. The parking ramp of the Moorhead Center Mall flooded to the first level. The dike along the river flooded to within a foot of the top. The river running over the top of the railroad bridge pylons, nearly flooding out the Main Street Bridge, like the bridge between Grand Forks and East Grand Forks was flooded out.

Until this time, I had no concept of what the land was supposed to look like. I had been to Fargo–Moorhead many times, but I never paid attention to the river. I never paid attention to the land except to ignore it because there was nothing to look at, and I preferred to read myself to Fargo and back when my family would go. I had no reason to stare at fields as a kid. Driving across it and seeing the water overwhelming everything, I had nothing to compare it to. I didn't know what the normal level of the river should look like. I didn't know the hill that the kids used for sledding was the dike used to keep the river at bay. I just didn't think of it.

I found my perspective that fall, when I left Nevis for college. During those years, I found a favorite spot along the Red River, on the river side of the dike. Sometimes I think my perspective is backward, measuring what is supposed to be in contrast to my first impressions. Taking photographs down by the water, I would look up and see the tops of the trees behind the dike, and I would remember what it used to look like. As I think about it now, this was the best way to form an impression of the place. Measure what is by what it's not supposed to be, and you'll come closer to what a place actually *is* at its core. Even now, years after college, when I go back to that place along the river or drive over the First Street Bridge and see the railroad pylons, time can't erase the memory of how close the river came to obliterating everything.

After the river crested in Fargo–Moorhead, all attention was focused on Grand Forks and East Grand Forks. On April 18, the Grand Forks dike failed. In the safety and dryness of my own home, I watched it happen. The memory is still chilling, all these years later. Only minutes before the water spilled over the top of the dike, there were people still sandbagging on top of it. On April 19, historic downtown Grand Forks caught fire. The irony was that the fire trucks could not put out the fire because the water was too deep for the trucks. Even if the trucks could get close, they couldn't use the fire hydrants. Eleven buildings burned in four-foot-deep floodwaters.

The only flood story I've heard in its entirety was that of Jon Schauer, although I have heard threads of other flood stories. My senior year of college, I sat next to Jon in band, and we fluted together. I had known Jon since my first day of college. He was of medium height, blond, played soccer and flute, a physics major from Grand Forks. I first heard the story of his family and the Flood in April 1998, a year after the waters receded.

Our house wasn't too far from the river. There is a good-sized coulee running through our backyard, but it is not part of the river. The house is on the bank of this coulee, and around the back of the house we'd built a clay dike up to about fifty feet. That doesn't mean that the dike was fifty feet high; it means that it would be good as long as the river didn't get above fifty feet. Flood stage in Grand Forks/East Grand Forks is twenty-eight feet; that means twenty-eight feet from the bottom of the river. We figured we'd be all right, since the river was predicted to crest at forty-eight feet. Believing in strength in numbers, twelve of my friends and I had skipped school for about a week and a half, going around town and sandbagging houses.

Everything was as good as could be expected until Wednesday morning, April 16, when my dad called my buddy's house to say that the sewer had backed up at our house. I didn't even have to ask my friends to help; they were already there. Four of us started in, carrying buckets of sewage-soaked stuff out of the basement. The sump pump was still going, but the sewer had backed up into our basement. It took all day to clean up the basement, and then we all went back into town for the night.

The next day, Thursday, my dad called us all back out to the house because crest predictions were rising, and we needed to build up our dike. The water was rising about an inch every hour, so four of us went to my house about nine that morning. Before the coulee had gone over the road, taking out the only remaining road to our house, the city had dumped fifteen dump truck loads of sandbags on our side of the island, sandbags that had to be shared by everyone on that island. We were getting to and from the house by boat.

When our dike was high enough, my buddies and I went to the neighbor's house to help fix their dike, which was starting to break. By noon, a half dozen more of my friends had arrived, so we could help more people. We sandbagged at my neighbors' houses, took stuff out of their basements, and sandbagged at my house. With all of us there, it didn't take long for that pile of sandbags to disappear and the anxiety to reappear. Someone took the pontoon across the road and brought back empty sandbags, and we started filling bags by hand from a pile of sand that my neighbor wasn't using.

On Friday all twelve of my friends came back, and we did much the same thing as we had the day before. My brother arrived by early afternoon, and we used his truck and trailer to fill the sandbags and deliver them around the island. After that, a group of forty people came and stayed for a good four hours. We definitely needed the help; my friends and I had started sandbagging at nine that morning and didn't stop until ten that night. It was only then that we could safely take a break. I slept for a couple of hours, but most of my friends stayed awake.

Late on Friday night, the river became jammed with sheets of ice. No one could get a boat across, so we were all stranded on our island. My brother woke us all up about three on Saturday morning and told us we needed to start sandbagging: the river was rising again. So, in the dark, aided only by lights from the house, we sandbagged from three until at least eight in the morning. The river was rising faster than we could slap sandbags onto the dike, but by early Saturday morning, the jam had passed, and we could take a breath without worrying that we would lose the battle while we did.

Most of the city had already been evacuated, and the National Guard was starting to evacuate the rest of the city. Most of my friends left on Saturday morning to be with their families. Then fifteen of my brother's fraternity brothers showed up. It was a miracle because they were huge, filled with fresh energy, and I'd been sandbagging for three straight days. It was enough of a miracle that I could get a few hours of sleep. When I woke up, we'd run out of sand. If we could have had one more row of sandbags, we might have been fine.

The river crested a few days later at fifty-four feet, and our dike was about fifty-three and a half feet. Our four sump pumps had been going twenty-four hours a day, and they needed gas. We needed food, most of which was provided by the Red Cross. We had been making several trips a day into town for gas and food. Eventually, all the gas stations closed. The people power was exhausted. There was no more sand. About five on Saturday afternoon, my dad decided we couldn't do any more. Most people don't know that you just can't slap one more sandbag on top of a dike to get those last six inches, that you have to build it up from the bottom.

The hardest thing I've ever had to do was open up a hole in the dike and let the water flood the house. If we hadn't done that, the force of the water coming through a broken dike would have destroyed everything in its path. We'd seen it happen before to too many people. That was Saturday, and the river didn't crest until Monday. Imagine using all the energy in your body you can possibly muster for as long as you possibly could and then having to give up. That's what made it so hard. To do that much and it is not enough.

One of the friends who helped sandbag my house, as well as many others, had lost his house at the beginning. He kept fighting, sandbagging nonstop at my house for a day and a half. I remember when my brother woke all of us up at three on Saturday morning, and this friend was crying. I'd never seen him cry before; after all, it's not something that eighteen-year-old boys often do. But he looked at me and said, "I've been fighting this for a week, and I just want to win one. I just want to win one." He'd lost nearly everything he owned after his dike broke, but he and his sister continued to fight for people they knew as well as people they didn't.

So many people came in to help, busloads of people we'd never met before. They worked so hard, doing something that we can't ever pay them back for. They came into our house, these

people we'd never met, people who didn't even have time to in-
troduce themselves. They came; they sandbagged. Every now and
then they'd have a bite to eat or something to drink, and then
they'd go right back to sandbagging. I remember my mom sitting
in the garage, and sometimes she'd just break down crying, be-
cause people she'd never seen before would be sandbagging our
house, come in, grab a soda, and go right back to sandbagging.
They came and did all that to help us, and we still couldn't beat
the river.

Even superlatives seem inadequate—Flood of the Century, a five-hundred-year flood, Flood of the Millennium.
But we don't have any other words; we have no other way
to understand, so we use what we have, and we rely on
numbers. The National Weather Service predicted a crest
of 49 feet in Grand Forks, but it eventually crested at 54.1
feet. Written in mud on a ruined house: *49 feet, my ass.* Of
the 2,500 homes in East Grand Forks, only 27 were not
damaged.

The *Grand Forks Herald* was flooded out, moving
their newsroom to the University of North Dakota until
that was flooded, then to Manvel Elementary School.
They did not miss one day of production, and in 1998
they won a Pulitzer for their coverage. At the site of the
rebuilt *Herald,* a clock tower stands ninety-seven feet
high, to commemorate the year of the flood.

Eleven buildings burned in downtown Grand Forks.
In the park created in that place, on a pile of bricks from
the burned-out Securities Building, stands a flagpole that
is fifty-four feet high, the height at which the Red finally
crested.

My current students were only two years old when

the flood happened, and their standards of floods—those who are from this area—lean toward 2009. I tried to tell them what it felt like to watch the Grand Forks dike fail, to see the incredible overland flooding around Fargo. I tried to articulate the difference between 1997 and 2009, that in 1997 we believed—as a result of our work ethic—that we could succeed as long as we worked hard. When we failed, it changed something fundamental in how we understood the world around us. In 2009, the numbers may have been worse in Fargo, but we knew beforehand that failure was a distinct possibility—that shift in thinking cannot be overstated in its importance.

Verbalizing any natural disaster ends up swirling around the truth, like rain around the eye of a hurricane. We know the truth is there, but there's a lot of heavy weather to get through first. Katrina has become the brand name in floods within the American imagination, but even so, those memories are fading. The 1993 Mississippi flood and the 2011 Missouri River flood were slow floods that were just as devastating as a flash flood. Neither can be controlled.

The floods caused by Hurricane Katrina brought back the 1997 Red River flood for many people, myself included. I heard about the dikes breaking in New Orleans and I went back to 1997. I watched parts of New Orleans burn and saw Grand Forks. I saw houses flooded to the eaves and saw Grand Forks. Toys floating down streets. Mountains of garbage. Mud-caked houses. Katrina was quick and unexpected in its severity, the failures of justice and social equality still a stain on the city and the government who failed to respond to the need. The 1997 Red River flood was slow and expected, but just as devastating. The greatest similarity between the two floods is that their soil was at one time under water. New Orleans is below sea level. The Red River floodplain was once the Glacial Lake Agassiz. Yet we find the concept of the land returning to its natural underwater state unnatural.

The frequency of Katrina stories has slowed to nearly nothing, but the stories are still being told—as they should be. Literature of Katrina is appearing on bookshelves, most fascinatingly in the genre of crime literature, from James Lee Burke's *Tin Roof Blowdown* to Joy Castro's *Hell or High Water,* offering a different tone of voice to the stories of Katrina. Eleven years before the 1997 Red River flood, Barry Lopez writes:

> Over time, small bits of knowledge about a region accumulate among the local residents in the form of stories. These are remembered in the community; even what is unusual does not become lost and therefore irrelevant. These narratives comprise for a native an intricate, long-term view of a particular landscape. And the stories are corroborated daily, even as they are being refined upon by members of the community traveling between what is truly known and what is only imagined or suspected. Outside the region this complex but easily shared "reality" is hard to get across without reducing it to generalities, to misleading or imprecise abstraction. *(Arctic Dreams: Imagination and Desire in a Northern Landscape)*

We who were there—even on the fringes—tell our stories and listen to the stories of those who actually felt the floodwaters. I'll tell stories of not being able to feel my hands, even in mittens, dropping the sandbags, not being able to hang on to them as I took them from the arms of the person next to me and passed them to the person on the other side of me. Of friends cracking jokes. Of being inside the Fargo Civic Center years later, not sure why I recognized the place, but eventually realizing this was the flood headquarters. I listened to Jon Schauer tell his story; I listened to my college professors tell their stories.

Lopez isn't specifically writing about disaster narratives, but the concept still fits. Disaster narratives form the bedrock of a community, how that community shapes its identity, how it comes to understand what it means to live in that place. Just as it's important to know that where I live in Nebraska was peripherally affected by the 1811–12 New Madrid earthquakes or that the volcanic ash that resulted in the Ashfall Fossil Beds exists, it's important to know the stories of flooding on the Red River—how else can we know where we live and who we are if we do not know what is under our feet? Lopez continues: "The perceptions of any people wash over the land like a flood, leaving ideas hung up on the brush, like pieces of damp paper to be collected and deciphered. No one can tell the whole story." The flood imagery resonates, as so many library books and historical records needed to be collected, preserved, or discarded—and then deciphered. Even mentally compiling the flood stories on top of each other will result in a clearer picture of the whole. It will never be an accurate picture, but it will be close. Strings of narrative come together to create a stronger rope.

Threads here don't form a quilt, but a rope. A binding metaphor. Midwesterners have a curious sense of community responsibility that they don't often realize they possess, let alone know how it affects their daily lives, because either it is invisible to us or we deliberately ignore what does not support that narrative. The culture of the Midwest has changed significantly in the past decades, with new refugee communities landing in Lincoln, Nebraska; Fargo, North Dakota; and the Twin Cities. After English and Spanish, the third-most-spoken language in Minnesota is Hmong, and Minneapolis is the second-largest community of refugees fleeing the civil war in Liberia, yet our perception remains that of a Scandinavian demographic.

These communities depend on each other, because the threads of narrative cannot exist on their own. The narratives always exist in relation to the threads around them. It is the reason my hometown of Nevis eats out on so many weekend evenings at benefit dinners for people we have never met or buy benefit raffle tickets for things we don't really want or need. People won't ask for help, but help will be offered because that is the way our community works. Help is a statement, not a question. We don't ask for it, but we get it when we need it. An example: The youngest son of my parents' good friends was born with spina bifida. Their oldest son was in my youngest sister's class at school. I'm sure the medical bills were hefty, but this kind of personal business is never discussed. It's none of our business, after all. Every summer when I was growing up, the community put on a Fine Arts choral concert and a freewill offering was taken to benefit someone who needs it. The choir themselves took suggestions and voted who the offering should go to. As a kid, I remember how beastly hot it was every year and how much I just wanted the singing to be over, so we could all get to the ice-cream social afterward. But I also remember how packed the church was, the largest space available to hold the concert, how the heat was as much body heat as it was July humidity in Minnesota.

I forget how many years the benefit offering went to these friends. They never asked for it, but the community gave anyway. Years later, the father of that family had health issues of his own, and again, the Fine Arts benefit supported them. Right now, as I write this, their sons are all grown, graduated from college, and the middle son is married with a year-old son of his own and one on the way. Last night, my mother called to say she just got an e-mail that the middle son's wife is in Fargo, in the hospital, with complete placenta previa, and they'll keep her there until they take the baby by C-section. But she's only twenty-four weeks along. I suspect that my parents, who live halfway between Nevis and Fargo, will provide a stopping point, a resting place, for any of that family who need it.

Those in the Red's path needed our help, and we could help them, so we did. We didn't do it expecting anything in return. It's in that way that individual threads of narrative are twisted into a rope. Expecting something in return, always having an ulterior motive for helping, unravels the rope. And that's not the way we function—or it's not the way we like to think we function.

My first adult experience with this concept was almost a full year after the 1997 flood. Minnesota often sees tornadoes, but rarely are they more than F1 or F2, and even more rarely do they strike outside the summer months. In March 1998 an F3 tornado leveled much of St. Peter, Minnesota, and we went to help Gustavus Adolphus College. Gustavus was one of the colleges in our conference, private and Lutheran, just like Concordia, where I attended.

This was my freshman year of college. A lot of the

Concordia sentiment was to help repay Gustavus for all the help they'd given Concordia the year before with the flood. I went, even though I had nothing to repay. I had two hands and no reason not to go. I wouldn't understand until I moved to Washington State the sense of community responsibility that permeates midwestern culture and that my reaction to both the flood and the tornado was ingrained and instinctive, native to the place where I grew up.

As we drove into the town of St. Peter, I was again faced with the same reaction I had the year before when seeing the flood. Here was the place on its worst day, and I didn't have anything to compare it to. I didn't know what it was supposed to look like. I saw a pair of hockey skates tangled in the branches of a tree. I saw signs of thanks painted on pieces of particleboard. *Our trees are gone, but our roots are still here.* I saw trees blown over at odd angles. Many of the fallen trees had already been sawed off at the roots, leaving the root systems half out of the ground. Some had already been taken out, leaving bomblike craters. Some trees had been blown over completely, some were only bent, some looked like there hadn't been a storm at all. I'd never seen anything like it, and I hope to God I never do again, but I know that's impossible. This will happen again.

We were assigned to work on the campus; we registered and were given work gloves. The crews took no chances with safety—we were told to stay fifty feet away from the buildings, since bricks and debris were still falling. Gloves were to be worn at all times because there was so much scattered glass. We cleaned some in Gustavus's Arboretum, raking around the remaining trees and clearing debris from the tree line. Some holes were marked with a twisted sign where there had once been a tree donated in someone's memory. Most of what we found were construction materials—shingles, tar paper, and particleboard. Occasionally we'd find a broken Lego or a picture of a family on vacation.

At the healing service later that afternoon, the campus pastor told us that when he first walked into the chapel after the storm, the eternal flame was still burning. Giving up was not an option. Not for the Gustavus students, not for the residents of St. Peter, not for any of the people who came to help. Those searching for survivors in the rubble of the World Trade Centers and the Pentagon didn't know how to give up—and stories like these abound in any kind of tragedy. This is what we want to remember, how the community banded together to help those who needed it. After 1997, after 9/11, after Katrina, we will always be torn between wanting to forget what happened and wanting to remember the support from thousands of nameless people. To forget would mean dismissing the help from unnamed strangers. To forget would mean unraveling the rope.

As the flood fades from my conscious memory, it is buried in my subconscious yet resurrected at odd and unexpected moments. It's not like I'm trying to forget. But somewhere in the mental image of what the Red looked like in 1997 and what it was supposed to look like, the flood, which didn't affect me personally, became internal. I feel like I'm appropriating the story of someone who has more of a right to tell it than I, but the flood is still inside me. It has certainly affected how I see Fargo–Moorhead, so how exactly does a flood distort our idea of place and how we connect to those places? Is our connection destroyed? Is it created? Is it washed clean?

It messes with our minds and how we deal with

such a thing—what doesn't kill us doesn't always make us stronger. Sometimes it breaks us into pieces so small that they cannot ever be put back together. Even so, everyone I've ever talked to about the flood, those who were there, has said something to the effect that what they lost was just *stuff*. Nobody died. *Stuff* can be replaced. The irreplaceable stuff, the pictures and yearbooks and heirlooms, hurts more, but it's still *stuff*. The pain of losing pictures and yearbooks and heirlooms is not in the loss of the physical pieces, but losing the memories those things hold. We don't need to remember every story that our past has to tell, because Grandma's table and the Christmas pictures from when we were little will hold those memories so we don't forget. They're tangible reminders of what we want to remember. But when those pieces are gone, all we have left is the rope of the narrative. We still have something.

Emotional forging is not what I'm after. The Red broke some people, and it didn't break others. Some people moved away, some people stayed. But I want to know how differently we relate to our places in the wake of something like the Flood. I imagine one's relationship to a recently flooded place is much different than with a place that has recently seen a wildfire or an earthquake or a tornado. While one may not always be able to see a wildfire coming, earthquakes and tornadoes and the like appear with relatively no warning; if you're in the path, your house and possessions are usually obliterated. With a flood, the possessions are still there. We watched the Red rise for weeks. We knew we were going to have a terrible flood, and we couldn't do anything to stop it. It was just water. It wasn't like fire, which destroys. It wasn't intangible like an earthquake. It wasn't a force like a hurricane. It was just water. We should have been able to control it.

Certainly a flood messes with our perceptions, with what a place should look like and what it does look like. My view of my favorite photo spot is changed, just because I can see the Red trickling in its normal state, and I can see it up to the top of the dike. But I'm not interested in how our view of a place changes. I want to know how the relationship changes. How do you look at the Red, how do you look at Fargo–Moorhead, Grand Forks–East Grand Forks, or any of the small towns and farms destroyed, differently from how you did before the winter of 1996–97? How can you look at the Red River without knowing that that simple combination of hydrogen and oxygen completely beat every ounce of human will we could muster? The simple answer is you can't.

And so perceptions continue to shift. We think of water as being clean, a cleansing agent. But the Red was chocolate brown during those weeks before and after the river crested, churning with the rich silt of the Agassiz lake bed. The water was not clean. When the river crested, then receded, everything was covered in mud.

The Red, during those weeks, was not simply water. It was not simply anything. It was a mixture of water and land, not just the water, not where water meets land. The land is as mortal as we are. We may view it as stoic and unchanging, much like the Scandinavians who settled it, but the land is fragile and sensitive. It can be changed drastically, but the reality is that the land is neither created nor destroyed; it is just changed. We must twist our threads into a rope and then tie the rope in knots, so that the narrative, the community, the memory will never come loose. Because one day, the Red will have a floodplain all its own.

The Canoe

1862

This is the year Nebraska became Settler Nebraska, the year that the white government in Washington thought they could turn the Great American Desert into the Breadbasket of the World just by legislation and blind ambition. Mostly, it worked, changing how the story of the Heartland would be written with four incredibly earth-shattering pieces of lawmaking: the Homestead Acts, which encouraged settlement of the Great Plains, farming a land that was never meant to be farmed; the Morrill Act, which established land-grant colleges, including the University of Nebraska, where I now sit, as well as the University of Minnesota my grandfather attended; the Pacific Railroad Act that changed the story of our movement across this place from feet and hooves to wagons and rails; and the establishment of the U.S. Department of Agriculture. The very fabric of the Plains would be changed from grasslands to farmlands. While physical movement to—and through—the Plains was important to get the country to where we wanted to be, the time had come to settle down, dig in, and plant a foundation. That goal became synonymous with the character of the Great Plains.

2012

My father, up north in Minnesota, e-mailed this morning and asked for the recipe to Al Goedtel's secret wood finish. I hesitated over the keyboard and wondered if Al was still alive—he was old when I was a teenager—and though I had been entrusted to keep the wood-finish recipe a secret, I wondered if his death would fall under the same rule as a secret recipe my father had been entrusted to keep. Marie's seasoned salt was famous where I grew up, and she was a widow with no children, no one to pass the recipe on to. My father wrangled the recipe out of her one day, with the promise that he would keep it secret until she died. He did. I wondered if I was bound by the same laws of trust. In the end, I gave my father the recipe, a specific combination of mineral oil, linseed oil, turpentine, and the white of an egg. It's how Al and I finished the two black walnut footstools I made with him in high school and the ash rocking chair. The varnish we used on the mahogany cabinet will eventually deteriorate, but not Al's finish.

Al Goedtel was one of the most interesting people I have ever known; it was a relationship between a high school girl and an old German cabinetmaker that started when my father brought me to Al's shop to make peg games for the upcoming church fund-raiser. He was in his midseventies when I knew him, but not too long ago he died as a bitter, abusive man who barely resembled the person I knew. He was always cranky, but that crustiness was actually one of the personality traits I enjoyed, because it always seemed like just bluster. Maybe abuse was always part of him and I never saw it, maybe it was Alzheimer's or dementia or some other quantifiable explanation. But I heard stories after his wife, Dorothy, divorced him—when they were in their eighties—and I started to wonder what other things I never saw, if Dorothy's tears the day she told me that Al was angry with my father and thus did not want to have anything more to do with me were part of a larger pattern I couldn't put together until much later. He made her tell me—he never told me himself. It is still difficult to reconcile the Al I knew with these realities, these memories, the way I understood the story of our friendship.

In the year that the Great Plains observes the 150th anniversary of so many history-shifting acts, Minnesota also observes the anniversary of the U.S.–Dakota War of 1862, and it makes me think of Al. The Minnesota Historical Society constructed an incredible exhibit on the war, the broken promises and treaties, the aftermath that still resonates today. For me, visiting the exhibit, the most potent aspect was the Truth Recovery Project, modeled on the process used in Belfast: "The term 'truth recovery' may imply that there is a single truth about what happened before, during and after the U.S.–Dakota War of 1862. In fact, there are multiple, often conflicting, interpretations about what happened, why it happened and who was responsible." The important thing is that there is no one truth; there is no one story.

1993

This is the date on the inside of my black walnut footstool. My sisters have its twin, functioning as a coffee table and footstool in their living room. I dream in black walnut, the silk of the grain. If I could only work in black walnut for the rest of my life, I would. When Al started to teach me carpentry, woodworking that he had turned into its own art form, he taught me what he called "old Indian tricks." Sometimes he would lick his finger and rub the wood, telling me that is how it would look when it was finished, and then he would tell me about the old Indian he had learned these tricks from, an Ojibwe man from Mille Lacs called Tom Benjamin by the whites.

Al learned his craft the old way, by building on a stick. I Googled the term, but came up empty. I used to have the stick we used to build my little mahogany cabinet, but it has been lost over the course of several moves. The concept is simple: four sides of a stick are marked with the measurements for length, height, and width. The idea is that you could reproduce a project an infinite number of times if you had the stick, a process I assume predates measuring tapes and literacy. Al made a series of black walnut grandfather clocks for his children and stepchildren, each identical because they were built on a stick.

While we made sawdust, he told me stories. Some were of Tom Benjamin and how he helped Al restore a birch-bark canoe that had survived the Sioux Uprising, around New Ulm, Minnesota, in 1862.

1955

After my grandfather finished his master's degree at the University of Minnesota, my grandparents and toddler mother moved to New Ulm, Minnesota, an overwhelmingly German town formed at the confluence of the Minnesota and Cottonwood Rivers. They would have known the history of the Dakota Uprising in 1862, would certainly have been a part of the centennial, but both grandparents are gone and I cannot ask them. I grew up climbing the steps to the top of Herman the German, sitting in front of the Glockenspiel with my grandparents and sisters. But New Ulm was a five-hour drive from where we lived in northern Minnesota, so it was easier for my grandparents to visit us than to pack three little girls in the car. By the time my grandparents moved north to the Cabin in 1991, my memories of the area had faded nearly completely. In the mid-1990s, on a family camping trip, we stopped in New Ulm because I wanted to visit the Brown County Historical Society to see the birch-bark canoe that Al had restored in the 1960s, the story of which was nearly as strong for me as the furniture we built.

1862

The story of Al's canoe begins with the same kind of warning that Edna O'Brien begins her novel *House of Splendid Isolation*: "History is everywhere. It seeps into the soil, the subsoil. Like rain, or hail, or snow, or blood. A house remembers. An outhouse remembers. A people ruminate. The tale differs with the teller." There is no one truth, no single story, and the best stories and truths are grounded in the tangible. The 1862 U.S.–Dakota War— I will choose to use the term the Minnesota Historical Society uses—was, perhaps, inevitable. Broken treaties and broken promises, a bad harvest in 1861, starving people forbidden to hunt off the reservation, and government payments to the Dakota held up while the Senate debated whether to pay in paper currency or gold. The Civil War raged elsewhere. Andrew J. Myrick, a storekeeper, reportedly told a group of hungry Dakota seeking credit: "If they are hungry, let them eat grass!" On August 17, a desperate, starving Dakota hunting party killed a white family. New Ulm was attacked twice, becoming a site of refuge for those fleeing other battles.

Over the course of the next six weeks, combat raged between the Dakota and the army. Andrew Myrick was found among the dead, his mouth stuffed with grass, or so the story goes. Reports vary widely as to the death toll, but it could be as high as seven or eight hundred whites; death tolls among the Dakota have never been established. The army responded swiftly, arresting nearly four hundred Dakota and sentencing 303 of them to death. President Lincoln commuted the sentence for all but thirty-eight, and that mass execution still remains the largest in United States history. The Dakota were banished from Minnesota, culminating in military campaigns and skirmishes that would not end until the massacre at Wounded Knee in 1890.

In an April 11, 2013, *New York Times* article, the former chairman of the Cheyenne River Sioux Tribe, Chief Joseph Brings Plenty, remembers stories of the massacre being handed down by the elders. But the physical site of Wounded Knee is another matter entirely: "The Wounded Knee site passed from the Oglala into private hands through the process known as allotment, begun in the late 1800s. . . . The idea was to shift control of our land from the collective to the individual and to teach the Lakota and other Native Americans the foreign notion of ownership. But to us, the policy was just another form of theft. The private owner of the Wounded Knee site, who has held title to the 40-acre plot since 1968, wants to sell it for $3.9 million. If the Oglala of Pine Ridge don't buy it by May 1, it will be sold at auction."

1962

This is the way that Al told me the story of the canoe. This is how I imagine it.

In 1962, the canoe was in the possession of a man named G. R. Kingham of Faribault. I had heard about it for years, how it had been passed down in his family from one generation to the next since the Uprising, but Kingham himself never knew how it had gotten into his family's possession in the first place. When I saw it for myself the first time, it was hanging from the rafters in his barn, the wind whistling through holes in the birch bark. Clearly, it was home to many different creatures.

"Have you ever tried to have it repaired?" I asked.

Kingham's face creased, an expression of embarrassment and pain. "I tried," he said, "but I couldn't find anyone to do it." Then he looked at me, jerked his chin from me to the canoe. "You're good with your hands—what would you do if you owned it?"

I shrugged. "I'd try to fix it."

He considered me for a moment. "If you promise to try to restore it and never let it out of your family, I'll sell it to you for ten dollars."

We shook hands and it was done. The challenge was a large one: the canoe itself, even in its state of neglect, was clearly the work of a master craftsman. It was seventeen feet long, made from one piece of bark, which had been spliced to cover the gaps. The sides were sewn together with a different kind of bark, the gunwales wrapped with root. The ribs and planking were of white pine, and the seams were pitched.

As punishment for the Uprising, the Sioux had been banished from Minnesota, so in 1962, my wife Mary Ann and eight-year-old son Bill made a trip to South Dakota to talk to the Sioux. But no one there knew anything about canoes, and it was suggested we talk to the Ojibwe, back home in Minnesota, on the Mille

Lacs reservation. At Mille Lacs, we knocked on doors, showed people pictures of the canoe, but nobody could—or would—help us. I wasn't terribly surprised. But in the course of our door-to-door search, we saw a tiny shack, camouflaged by trees. When I tried to talk to the elderly man who opened the door, he only shouted at me in a language I did not understand. Rage lit his eyes, and he gestured wildly for us to leave. So we did.

I was not discouraged. "We're going to go back to talk to him," I told Mary Ann.

The next day, when the old man opened the door, I stuck my foot in the space so it couldn't be closed. "All I want to do is talk to you," I said. Needing a cigarette, I took out the package and offered him one. The man took it warily.

I showed him the pictures and told him what a man down the road had said, something about finding the roots for the gunwales in the swamp.

The old man shook his head. "Spruce tree grow on hill, not in swamp."

He knew!

The old man cocked his head to the side, looked at me. Then he shook his head. "Not today. No, not today."

Silence hung thick in the air, thick like the smoke from our cigarettes. I resisted the urge to break it, to hurry the old man into telling me what I needed to do. "Have you had something to eat?" I finally asked. It was about noon, and we had brought our lunch with us.

"No."

"Would you like to eat with us?"

The old man's coal eyes sparked with surprise, but his wrinkled skin absorbed much of his reaction. He went to get his wife, who was hardly five feet tall and as wrinkled as her husband, and the five of us sat outside and shared sandwiches and coffee.

He said his name was Natamaquanape, but the white man

called him Tom Benjamin. His wife's name was Nabow. Whenever I asked him about his age, Tom's response was always, "Well, I'm over seventy." When he died a few years later, I figured he and his wife were past ninety, nearing the century mark.

Tom fingered the pictures of the canoe that I had brought. "Not our canoe. Sioux." The canoes have different shapes, he explained later. The ends of the Sioux canoe resemble the head of an eagle; the Ojibwe canoe is rounded at the ends. But it was clear that they were both made with the same principles, and he agreed to help me.

2012

I wish I knew if the qualities I ascribe to Tom and Al are accurate, how much ethnic bias and color Al added to the story as he told it over time. There is so much that I, as the reteller, assume about Al's motivations, about how the interactions between Tom and Al transpired. But I definitely see the stubborn German I knew in the man who simply would not leave Tom alone and stuck his foot in the door. I wonder if Al's offering of the cigarette was an accident rather than cultural sensitivity. Al never knew how to spell Tom's name in Ojibwe—and I don't either. It's the mistranslation of oral to written storytelling, so I spelled the name as Al pronounced it. But if Tom was in his nineties during the 1960s, he would have had to have been born during the fallout after the Uprising was crushed. Tom was not Dakota—he was Ojibwe—but in the larger scheme, that would not have mattered much. Neither group was treated well by the whites. For myself, I wonder what stories Tom had to tell.

The canoe itself was damaged, but still alive, still a testament to a violent era in American history, in Minnesota history, and even though my family had not immigrated yet, I still feel a measure of ethnic guilt in the events of the war. There are stories untold, woven into the roots that wrapped the gunwales, the bark that stitched the birch bark together.

1963–1968

Restoring the canoe took place in stages, limited by the seasons. In the winter, Tom taught me how to put the canoe back into shape. It was misshapen and twisted from years of neglect. Tom told me that I needed to heat the canoe, then reshape it. When it was heated, it became quite pliable—when cold, it became hard. I appreciated the ingenuity. I worked with wood for most of my life, building nearly everything on a stick, and Tom and I shared the belief that the old ways were often the best.

In the spring, we went to the woods, and he taught me how to gather the roots from spruce trees to replace the broken and rotten root around the sides of the canoe. The roots I needed, he said, were about the size of an old man's thumb. We wrapped them up, and then when we had time, we used a knife and sliced them down the middle. No matter how many crooks there were in the root, the knife always followed the center.

I also needed some birch bark to patch the sides of the canoe. He told me, "You can't get it in the winter. You must do it in the summer." The birch has a double bark, and the outside bark was what I needed. The next summer, he demonstrated how not to cut too deep and avoid hurting the tree.

That summer was also the summer of the pitching, to water-proof the seams of the canoe. Tom started by taking pieces of hard pitch from the trees, collecting them in a basket. We melted the hardened pitch in a kettle over a very slow fire and then strained it, since all the dirt and bark had sunk down to the bottom. When it cooled, it was a solid peanut-butter-colored chunk that would shatter if dropped. We melted the sap again and stirred in powdered charcoal and tallow. We mixed it to the right consistency, and then used it to waterproof the joints of the canoe.

The smallest pieces of bark were sewn together with basswood bark, and Tom taught me how to collect the inner bark from the thinner limbs of the basswood tree, not the trunk. After the piece was taken from the tree, it was easy to separate it into whatever size strand I needed.

Eleven white cedar ribs were missing from the bottom of the canoe. The planking was one-sixteenth-inch thick, half-lapped, like siding on a house. The ribs were driven in tight, using no nails or fasteners of any sort. After I straightened and cleaned it, I remade the missing ribs out of white cedar, just like the originals.

As I cleaned it, though, I noticed a hole on one side of the canoe, right above the water line, as big around as my pinky finger. Kingham, the man who had sold me the canoe, explained to me later that it was a bullet hole. The story, as he told it, is that during the Uprising, an Indian had been shot in it as he was going down the Minnesota River. Since I wasn't there that day, I can't tell you what happened, but I did notice a big, dark spot like dried blood on the bottom of the canoe, right under that hole. I tried to sand it, but I couldn't get rid of the spot. And I never did patch that hole.

2012

I found Tom Benjamin through the Minnesota Death Index. Or at least I assume it is him: born July 1, 1887; died December 31, 1968. I looked at those dates and wondered if they were made up, estimates along the lines of *he was born in the summer* and *he died during the winter.* I have tried searching for his wife, but I have no idea what her Anglo name was—and I have only an assumed spelling of Nabow. Genealogy is always a great treasure hunt for me, the tangible records of a life.

A phone call to the Brown County Historical Society confirmed that no one had done any research on the canoe—and these days it is in storage, no longer on display—and all they know about it is what the Goedtel family told them when they donated the canoe. I have no way of knowing if the bullet-hole story is true or if Kingham accidentally punched a hole in it with a rake handle. Or if the bloodstain was animal, not human. But it is another way that we create native history, by speculation, which is its own kind of false story.

1985

Twenty years passed between the finishing of the canoe and Tom's death. Mary Ann had passed away, and I had remarried. Dorothy and I were thinking of moving north. I didn't have room for the canoe and neither did my son Bill, but I had promised Kingham to keep it in my family. Eventually, we made arrangements with the Brown County Historical Society in New Ulm for the canoe to be displayed in their new Indian exhibit. The canoe still belongs to my family, but it is on permanent loan. I couldn't even get insurance for it—only for the value of a used canoe.

It took a big crane to get it up and through the second-story window of the museum, and it was quite a spectacle. I remembered the look on Tom's face when I first met him, the excitement of all that time spent in the woods. I remembered his tiny wife, beating the hell out of his kinikinik, his preferred tobacco of red willow. I remembered the last time I saw him, before he died.

2012

The only time I saw the canoe, I was in my early teens. I don't have much cause to be in New Ulm anymore, no reason to visit except for curiosity. The Dakota Hotel, built in 1858, served as a hospital and refuge during the 1862 war, but it was demolished in 1972. I have fuzzy memories of various places, and I wonder what they would look like now. I have this feeling that when I return, I will ignore the buildings and sit for a while on the shores of the Minnesota River. I will imagine a blistering August day, the sounds of screams and gunfire, and a story I will never know, sliding down the river in a birch-bark canoe.

Deadwood

The story of the West is the story of hope. Of hope so insistent that it compelled movement over large distances. Of hope so pervasive that it soaked the Plains soil like rain. Of hope so tangible that it rose higher than the Rockies, driven up by cataclysmic forces, for nothing worth dreaming comes without a price. Of hope so expansive that it became the air, inhaled and exhaled, until it pushed through the atmosphere and collided with the stars and brought them down, close enough to touch.

Boot Hill is filled with dreamers.

The road leading up to Mount Moriah Cemetery in Deadwood, South Dakota, is a 20 percent grade. During our summer family vacations, contests between the drivers—Mom and Dad—fell into two categories: who could hit the most road construction (extra points were awarded for delays) and who could drive the steepest grade. These contests were not skill-based but rather based on who happened to be driving at the time. Currently Dad holds the grade record, unchallenged since the first and only time our family visited Deadwood, back in the early nineties. When I was twenty-four, I tied the record by driving the road myself. I was alone.

Most brave the grade to stand in the presence of history, to stare at the graves of Wild Bill Hickok and Calamity Jane, to bask in the literal *story* of the West, the mythology that this place created. On this trip, I was not distracted by the wonder I felt as a twelve-year-old, the last time my feet tramped this soil. This time I was much more cognitively aware of the way the houses were built into the gulch, of what Main Street looked and felt and smelled like, of the Adams Museum, of the layout of Mount Moriah Cemetery. On the steep sides of the gulch, I noticed the burned sticks that used to be trees, remnants of a massive forest fire the year before—people had been afraid they would lose the town, but the fire stopped before it got there. During my first trip to Deadwood, I was consumed by the romance of the Old West, of whatever intangibles made the place what it was. At the age of twelve, I didn't notice or care about the slot machines or the annoying pervasiveness of the gambling. I wanted to run my hands over the rough wood of the saloon doors, wanted to be a witness to the trial of Jack McCall, the man who shot and killed Wild Bill—who was subsequently acquitted. I wanted to strap on a six-shooter and be famous. I wanted to know Calamity Jane, watch her chase after Wild Bill. I didn't question these stories. I was peripherally aware that my grandmother was searching for information on her grandfather, Charles McAllister, but it didn't make much impression on me, mostly because at the time, my two sisters and I were trying to be invisible, the kind of grandchildren our grandparents seemed to want.

This time, I asked the questions I needed to ask, even though I still wanted to strap on a six-shooter. Inside Mount Moriah's gates, I walked past Wild Bill and Calamity Jane toward Charles and Ferne McAllister. As I passed the gravestones of young and old, male and female, I wondered how many people buried at Mount Moriah died "with their boots on"—violently—a saying that gave rise to nicknaming cemeteries of the American West "Boot Hill."

Charles and Ferne are my blood, but that connection isn't enough to make me care about them as people. Since I was the the family historian, part of my visit was easily explained as genealogy, but in all honesty, that couldn't explain the entirety of my trip through Deadwood. Charles Henry McAllister was born in New Hampshire in 1873 to Charles Edward and Ida McAllister. I have not yet discovered why the McAllisters left the East, but likely the hope for something better played a large role. Hope for something different, hope for something beyond their wildest imaginings. Wild, indeed. Bill Kittredge, in *Owning It All,* wonders, "What compelled men [and women] to believe promises of paradise on earth with such simple-minded devotion? Well, for openers, a gut yearning for the chance of becoming someone else, and freedom from the terrible weight of responsibilities." Some people can be happy in the life they have always known. Some people do find their niche in small places. But some people find any collar too tight, and what wouldn't be tempting about a place where you could be anyone you wanted to be, a place where nothing existed except possibilities? Of course, thinking of only the positives of the West probably landed most of these emigrants six feet under, because you can never underestimate a place that provokes such a mythology, where stories grow as tall as the wheat—unless drought or tornadoes or something else shrivels the wheat into dust. It is the mythology—and the lure of the mythology—that is important.

I needed more concrete information.

Charles Henry McAllister married Ida Smith in 1896 in Deadwood, and they welcomed their first children—twin girls—on July 27, 1897. Ferne and Kayo, the hope for the next generation. (Edna was born in 1899.) But at the age of five weeks, Ferne died. I don't know the specifics. My grandmother, Kayo's daughter, recalls that the only thing her mother said about her twin was that Ferne was a sickly child. Deadwood death records don't start until 1905, a year before Charles died, so all I have of Ferne is a gravestone bearing her name at Mount Moriah and a photograph taken no more than a few days before she died. I may never know any more about her. I don't like these brick walls. Running into them hurts.

Charles does not have a death certificate, as such, but all the necessary information is contained in a very large leather-bound book in the records office. The information from this book is contained in a database, so I searched for "Charles McAllister" and came up with nothing. I looked at the McAllisters that came up and saw that the dates for "Ira McAllister" matched my Charles. I went to look at the book itself and realized that whoever had entered the information in the computer had transcribed the swirly handwriting of *Chas* as *Ira*.

Charles died on October 6, 1906, at the age of thirty-three. Each piece of information that lists his cause of death is different, but whatever killed him was definitely lung related. Family mythology says that it was black lung disease from working the silver mines in Lead. Newspaper obituaries—of which there are many—call it consumption and note that he went to the southwest for a few months, but the drier air didn't help him. The official cause of death, what is written in the book of death records, is *fibroid phthisis,* tuberculosis. The death record lists the duration of his illness as a year. The obituaries say that he was police chief under Mayor McDonald, who was mayor of Deadwood in 1906, so Charles wasn't chief for very long. And if he was that ill, how did he become police chief in the first place?

In his final moments, did Charles regret that he couldn't be killed doing something heroic in the line of duty? What glory is there in tuberculosis?

Once I had finished in the records office, I walked next door, through considerable heat, to City Hall, where I inquired how I might find information about past police chiefs, the position Charles had held before his death. The woman sent me to Historical Preservation. I left Historical Preservation an hour or two later, leaving behind a very happy historian—Deadwood was redoing its police badges to look like the old ones, but they didn't have any pictures of them. I had a picture of Charles in his chief outfit, complete with badge. When I left, I hadn't found any more information about Charles, but I did know more about the McAllister house. And that was a step in the right direction.

Life in the West is nothing but a series of steps in the right direction.

Direction became important during my short time in Deadwood. The McAllisters lived in Deadwood during its heyday. Wild Bill Hickok was killed in 1876—Charles would have been only three years old at the time, but even this late in the century, Deadwood was still wild. The Indian Wars, which had been raging since the Sioux Uprising in 1862 in Minnesota, continued until the massacre at Wounded Knee and "the closing of the American West" around 1890. Deadwood had everything a wild frontier town needed: characters whose legends were larger than they were, lawlessness in spite of the law, where truth and fact were more often than not unclear, like watching distant objects under the hot sun—shimmers and blurs. Bill Kittredge writes in *Owning It All,* "The mythology of the American West is also the primary mythology of our nation and part of a much older world mythology, that of lawbringing." It follows that my interest should center on Charles's profession of police chief in Deadwood. But this is only one element of the story, and a small one, at that. It is the relationship of story and place that fascinates me first and foremost.

Any place can have lore attached to it. There is nothing remarkable about that. What I am after, what I am searching for—at the root—is more complex. The Irish have a term for this: *dinnseanchas,* which translates to place-lore. I want to know how landscape shapes mythology and what kind of people grow in that kind of soil. There is a different flavor to the *dinnseanchas* of the East Coast, the Deep South, the Old West, the gold rush countries of California and Alaska.

The American West—old and new—has more of its own lore and tradition than any other place I am familiar with. Deadwood, as an old town of the Old West, holds more *dinnseanchas* than some other places of the Old West, typified by larger-than-life characters, larger-than-believeable events, and a land that takes no pity on the stupid. The cowboys are always rugged, the pioneers are always rough and salt of the earth, the schoolteachers are prim, and the prostitutes have hearts of gold. But *dinnseanchas* is more than just stereotypes or stories, factual or invented—*dinnseanchas* is made up of the small stories that make a place what it is.

Remove the place from the story and you have no story.

The *dinnseanchas* of the West is the result of the space itself. Gretel Ehrlich, in *The Solace of Open Spaces,* the most honest painting of the *dinnseanchas* of the West, writes:

> We Americans are great on fillers, as if what we have, what we are, is not enough. We have a cultural tendency toward denial, but, being affluent, we strangle ourselves with what we can buy. We have to look at the houses we build to see we build against space, the way we drink against pain and loneliness. We fill up space as if it were a pie shell, with things whose opacity further obstructs our ability to see what is already there.

The perception is that the West was a land waiting to be filled—never mind that it was already filled with buffalo as far as the eye could see, vast prairies of grasses, mountains filling the eyescape. We could not see, or conveniently ignored, the people who were living there. They became part of the emptiness to be filled, as genocide progressed across the continent. The place was so vast that the absence of everything familiar to Easterners was attractive. They filled the place with what they could understand: stories. Stories of people and animals and places that were larger than their lives, larger than what anyone had previously dreamed. Stories that expanded to fill human potential and imagination. There were no boundaries in the West, physical or personal or imaginative. Would Wild Bill have made such a name for himself in Boston? Billy the Kid? Wyatt Earp? Probably not, since the West, in its uncivilized state, tends to scrape people down to the bedrock, where they find their last reserves of who they are. Sometimes the bedrock is shallow, and those people quickly find that the soil of the West makes a suitable grave, just as good as the soil back East. Sometimes the bedrock is deeper than they dreamed, but they have to get through the sod first.

In the West, anything was possible if you had the guts. *Go West, Young Man!* Manifest Destiny was the dream, after all. That was the beginning of the *dinnseanchas*. Without the people who went West, the *dinnseanchas* would never have developed—and there is an obvious intangibility to humanity. There would have been no one to tell the stories, no one to repeat and embellish. This is obvious. And the mythology grew, stories with little basis in fact: the facts could not be challenged, so imagination became fact. In how many places, in how many landscapes, is that shift possible? There is a brilliance to that idea that tends to blind me with wonder.

The McAllisters play a part as relative nonentities in the mythology of the place that is even larger than the role they play in the *dinnseanchas,* even though their names will never appear in any history books alongside Wild Bill Hickok and Calamity Jane. The McAllisters were there, present, alive, at the time; therefore they played a role in forming and perpetuating the mythology, in this case, the mythology of the mundane. Not all mythology has to be larger than life—life has to be established before it can be embellished.

The story of the West is the story of hope. Of hope for surviving the day, for surviving the winter. Of hope for not outliving your children. Of hope to watch your children grow. Of hope bubbling in the blood, so that each day is an exercise in determination, finding the reserves of your strength, learning who you are at the very deepest level. The story of the West is nothing without determination. Nobody would have survived otherwise.

No one can live on hope alone.

Stories always expand without tangibles, floating in the atmosphere, shifted by each gust of imagination. The mythologies of *dinnseanchas* are anchored to the place, giving them a clearer intersection between truth and fact. Otherwise, you are searching through the elements of the story, trying to figure out what is real and what is not, because the *dinnseanchas* is a way to find out what is real in a mythological landscape. The best stories, the ones that actually do something, are attached to specific places, specific physical landmarks, as if to anchor them in reality.

I had two tangibles left in Deadwood: Charles and Ferne's gravestone and the family's house. This was all that was left to convince me that the McAllisters were real and contributed to the life and mythology of Deadwood. I have photographs of the family in front of the house, taken in October 1906, only days before Charles died. Charles, sitting in a chair, looking very ill. His daughters Kayo and Edna and their dolls. No sign of Ida.

Because Deadwood is so concerned about preserving its past, physical and emotional, I thought it possible that their house might still be standing, but I learned it had been torn down between 1909 and 1915.

So I went back up to Mount Moriah and stood in front of the only tangible remains of the McAllister *dinnseanchas*. Charles and Ferne's gravestone is a waist-high column of gray granite. Ferne's information faces south:

Ferne A.
daughter of
Mr. and Mrs. C. H. McAllister
BORN
July 27, 1897
DIED
Sept 1, 1897

Standing there in the intense June sun, I try to see Charles, Ida, and Kayo around the grave at Mount Moriah and feel the tenor of their grief. I try to imagine Ida, dressed in black, holding baby Kayo, and I want to see the tears dripping off her chin onto the face of the baby. I want to see Charles, standing next to Ida, an arm around her waist, supporting himself as much as her. He is twenty-four years old, and she is twenty-three. No parent, whatever their age, is prepared to lose a child, but these two were so young. I want to see if there are tears on his cheeks, or if he stares blankly into the hole in the ground into which his daughter is being lowered. His daughter, blood of his blood.

Maybe I have the picture backward. Maybe Charles is crying and Ida's emotions cannot break through her stunned grief. Ferne was only five weeks old, but for nine months, Ida had carried her, felt those two additional hearts inside her. Was she awakened at night by a flying elbow or knee? Did Charles and Ida each have a favorite daughter? Whose favorite was Ferne? How much faith did they place in the hope that Ferne would survive to adulthood, even though she was frail? Or did they know she would die and hoped that God would take her quickly, before they got too attached to her? Maybe they weren't ready to handle two children; maybe they were grateful that Ferne died, even though such a thought would never have been voiced. Maybe it was a blessing.

Hope surrounds the birth of a child, joy surrounds the life of a child, agony surrounds the death of a child, and regrets surround the memory.

Charles's gravestone information is more scarce—and inaccurate. *Chas. H. McAllister, DIED Oct 2, 1906, AGED 33 years.* He actually died on October 6. I thought I felt more relief than grief on this side of the stone. Charles had been ill for a long time, and Ida's emotional reserves were probably tapped dry. Everything she had been was gone. She used to laugh, when she was younger, but she can't remember the last time she even smiled. She doesn't even cry anymore—that requires more emotion than she has. She doesn't feel dead inside, just dry. There are some days she doesn't even recognize herself.

This could explain a disturbing story I heard from my grandmother, Kayo's daughter. My grandmother reports that Ida was not a happy woman and intensely disliked Kayo's husband, Fred—but she never approved of any other man either. Apparently Edna didn't like men much either. I wondered if this had anything to do with Edna and Bud never having children, but when I asked Grandmother about it, she told me that Ida had always made a to-do about Edna being too frail for children, and when Edna had her appendix out, Ida had the doctors ensure that Edna would never have children. Is this true? I know that sterilizations happened with alarming regularity during the first decades of the twentieth century, but it adds to the composite picture of Ida that I am forming and how such a terrible decision might have been made by a mother for a daughter. Maybe Ida had seen what happened to frail girls who weren't strong enough to bear the children they carried, and she didn't want that to happen to her youngest daughter. Maybe she didn't want Edna to go through what Ida went through, losing Ferne. I don't know.

The challenge, when pursuing any land-based mythology, is to find the mythology and infer the facts—and the motivations. To work the stories in reverse, to find how the people were shaped by the stories. Part of this is basic curiosity, to discover who these people really were. Part of it is curiosity of a different kind: to look at them, then deliberately bounce our identities off our own landscapes and learn how we may be a product of our places. We can collect enough facts to fill a library, but those facts on their own do nothing to indicate what kind of human these people were. We can get closer only by reading between the lines, attaching motivations to actions, attaching emotions to decisions, attaching meaning to choices. To ask if we would have made the same choice under those circumstances. Under what circumstances would we sterilize our daughters? Under what circumstances would we take the choice of having children or not out of their hands?

The *dinnseanchas* of the West is a way to survive the West. Research has shown that some patterns are linked to genetics—alcoholism, obesity. We already know about survival of the fittest and survival techniques being passed down in our genes—stories of survival serve the same function. *Listen to the stories of those who came before and do not repeat their mistakes. Listen to how they succeeded and do the same. Listen to how they failed and avoid those thoughts and actions.* What other purpose would there be in telling these stories? If you told these western *dinnseanchas* stories in the East, it would be for entertainment. In the West, the stories have a different function. Entertainment may have been one element, but rarely are the stories confined to one level.

Losing a spouse is not a new concept, but there are as many reactions to this loss as there are people who experience it. Ida McAllister lived for forty-some years after Charles died, but on my mother's side of the family, Albert Olson died of a broken heart a month after his Josephine, his wife of sixty years, died of a stroke. I imagine that eastern Minnesota affected Albert after the loss of Josephine as much as Deadwood affected Ida after the death of Charles. Mostly, I think that Ida survived for one reason that is specific to the *dinnseanchas* of the West.

In the West, women needed a specific kind of strength to survive. Bill Kittredge writes in *Owning It All,* "This country fosters a kind of woman who never seems to bother about who she is supposed to be, mainly because there is always work, and getting it done in a level-eyed way is what counts most. . . . It is as though they wear down to what counts and just last there, fine and staring the devil in the eye every morning." Ida may have been a western girl when she married Charles, but Deadwood likely turned her into a western woman before long. How else would she have been able to survive the death of a child—and nine years later, the death of her husband? Would the girl she had been be capable of packing up everything she knew and moving to a place where she knew nothing, knew no one?

If Deadwood itself—and the West—played a role in Ida's reaction to Charles's death, she would have done exactly what she did: what needed to be done. This is another element of the *dinnseanchas* for women: practicality. She could wallow in her grief, pine for her husband taken so young, or she could remember that she was responsible not just for herself but two little lives besides. The West did not allow her the luxury of concentrating on herself. She took her doctor's advice to move to a different climate and went to San Diego, where she would have a better chance of not leaving her daughters orphans.

What I find most interesting about the *dinnseanchas* of the West is that it is not consistent. Most of California does not fall into the same land-based mythology. My theory is that because of the different climate, the warmer air, and the proximity to the ocean, the people who grew in this land had a different relationship with it. When Ida transplanted herself and her girls into the Southern California soil, it affected her. Suddenly she didn't have to worry so much about keeping the family warm and fed. Fruit grew on trees in their backyard. They didn't need wool in January. Things must have seemed easy for Ida, at least on a cellular level. This, I believe, is what led her to put her girls in a convent school and then basically abandon them for long periods of time. I have letters that Kayo wrote, wondering if Ida is going to come pick them up for Christmas. It's hard to like Ida during her time in San Diego, but I'm trying to understand how she could do what she did.

The story of the West is the story of hope. Of hope so invasive that the presence was cancerous, dangerous. Of hope so infectious that some did not survive. Of hope so beautiful that it was worth risking everything. Of hope for happiness, for contentment, for fulfillment, found wherever possible.

My great-aunt Katherine—Kayo's oldest daughter—gave me boxes of genealogical miscellany, and I couldn't be more ecstatic about it. I'm emptying them onto the living room floor and making a mess as I do. But contained in the boxes is a six-inch stack of letters from my great-grandfather Fred Ponsford, written to my great-grandmother Kayo before they were married. I don't think there is an alphabetic translation for the sound I make.

I settle down to read them.

I didn't know Fred at all, so this is all new. His letters are generally filled with news of his doings and his love and "thousands of kisses" to his darling Kayo. "The next time I see you, dear, I shall see what I can find this time for a little real kissing bee. Those we had this weekend were far too few, although I wouldn't give anything for the few we did have," he writes. It is hard to reconcile the general mushiness of his letters with the stern-looking man in the pictures I have.

My grandmother, Kayo's younger daughter, doesn't have much good to say about her father—and trying to pry anything out of her is difficult. In the cloudy, vague memories of early childhood, my father remembers Fred as a reserved, almost stern man. But they are both willing to talk about Kayo, describing her as the kindest, most gentle person they had ever known. She had a regal bearing, a person who would be willing to give the shirt off her back to someone who needed it. My father tells us how she encouraged her grandchildren to sell the mistletoe off her oak tree for spending money at Christmas. She was stunningly beautiful—something I can see for myself—even as she aged; her hair was dark, her eyes lit with simple joy, five-ten in height, slender of build. So I smile at the hoops she dragged poor Fred through en route to the "I do."

In setting out to find Fred through his letters, I find Kayo instead, the next link in the McAllisters of Deadwood. She was nine years old when she and her mother and sister moved to San Diego, and those formative years inside the *dinnseanchas* of the West would have formed her bones. How much remained after living in California is unknown.

Fred was born in England and immigrated to San Diego with his brothers and sisters around 1916. Before his immigration, Fred was enlisted in the Royal Air Corps. I have his enlistment papers. Why he left the British military and moved to San Diego during the height of the Great War, I don't understand. Nevertheless, Fred enlisted in the American air corps and became an airplane mechanic—he couldn't get an officer's commission because he was not an American citizen.

On leave, he met Miss Kayo McAllister at a dance and fell in love at first sight, as far as I can tell. How she felt about him initially isn't certain, since I have only his letters. I try not to think about Grandmother throwing away Kayo's letters—it hurts too much. It is apparent, though, that Fred felt a lot more for Kayo than she did for him—a few letters speak of the "cruel" way she was treating him:

Your letter I do not understand at all. If it was your intention to hurt me, you have succeeded very well. You could not have written anything that hurt more if you had tried. By the way, it reads your opinion of me is very small indeed. . . . I have written to you almost every day that mail has gone out from here, so I think your remark about writing once a week [was] very uncalled for. . . . You might least take into consideration our mail and phone service out here before you write such a bitter letter as this last one. Well, dear, I don't feel like writing any more now, so I will quit with the prospect of at least an utterly miserable day. So I will close hoping to find you as well as it leaves as ever tho' unhappy.

Your Own, Fred.

I felt guilty and I didn't even write the letter. As I dug through Katherine's boxes, I found that this wasn't the first time Kayo had done something selfish: before Fred, Kayo was apparently on the verge of marrying another man, and the letters I have indicate she didn't return the ring when he asked for it, not even when the man's sister wrote and said they needed the ring to pay their mother's doctor bills. That doesn't exactly go along with the kindhearted, gentle-to-a-fault Kayo that my father fondly remembers.

Good. I would be sorely disappointed if she was all sweetness and light—humanity is rarely that predictable. But given this scenario and these decisions she made, I want to know how much Deadwood played a role. She left Deadwood when she was nine years old, old enough to have formed impressions of the place and her place in it. Did she inherit this streak of practicality from Deadwood, from the West, not willing to settle for less than the man she wanted? Did she take from Deadwood the tendency to be a little selfish sometimes, because those who give everything all the time will never survive? Did she learn about doing what needs to be done? To take something for herself once in a while?

Too much time has passed since the McAllisters left Deadwood and since the West was officially considered closed for the stories that grow in that land to stay the same. This is a good thing. Part of this is population, part is technology, and part is simple time. The progression of the mythology has mostly gone beyond true *dinnseanchas* into something closer to home, something more emotional, and it is a mythology I have more wherewithal to question and interrogate. It doesn't matter that the mythology itself is no longer land-based, related to or influenced by place, because though the myth of the West still exists, that which gave rise to the *dinnseanchas* in the first place is no longer applicable. It is not so black-and-white out there anymore. The West is populated to the point where the stories that fill the space do not have the room to expand as they once did.

What is the next step in the evolution of a land-based mythology? What remains of Deadwood in my grandmother's DNA? My father's? Mine? Grandmother was born and raised in San Diego, as were my father and his siblings. They didn't need the stories of Deadwood to survive, so I think the stories became recessive. They were replaced by stories of Santa Ana winds, earthquakes, riptides, wildfires. My grandmother doesn't know anything of her mother's life in the West and shares very little of her growing-up, even when I ask. After my parents married, they moved to Mom's home state of Minnesota, and this is where my sisters and I were born and raised. My own *dinnseanchas* is not of the West but of the North—these stories form not only where I come from but who I am. These are the stories, the ethic of place, born of the land, that give me everything I need to survive physically, emotionally, mentally. These are the stories that connect me to the people around me, to where my blood finds its ideal temperature. These are my stories. But somewhere in my blood lie those recessive stories of the western *dinnseanchas*.

Back in Deadwood, surrounded by the excessive heat of that June afternoon, this place feels familiar. The town feels closed-in, but rather than feeling claustrophobic, it is comforting. Since *dinnseanchas* looks at how a place forms its stories, maybe the geography of the gulch itself played a role in not only forming the mythology but also holding on to the mythology long after the West was Won. Maybe the geography of the gulch holds the stories in, doesn't let them escape, doesn't let them spread out and evaporate, the way they might along a flatter terrain. Maybe this is Deadwood's greatest secret, the greatest value it has to offer.

The story of the West is the story of hope. Of hope for a life so different from what they had left behind that the settlers made choices they might not have made Back East. Of hope for life, so

determined to live, that they deliberately prevented life. Of hope for a land that would feed them, shelter them, become part of them. Of hope for a permanence as solid as the mountains, continuous as the Plains, all-encompassing as the ocean.

Boot Hill is filled with dreamers.

Petrography

S cant feet from my toes, the world drops off. I'm staring across the canyon created by the Missoula Floods
toward Dry Falls in Washington State, intense sunlight
highlighting the water-formed cliffs. The sun turns the
small pools of water at the canyon base to bright, im-
probable blue, the color of my mother's eyes. Dry Falls,
I have learned, is the largest waterfall in the world, but it
hasn't been wet since the last time Glacial Lake Missoula
flooded, ten thousand years ago. When it was wet, it was
ten times larger than Niagara Falls—about 400 feet tall and
3.5 miles wide. It takes some imagination to see Dry Falls
overflowing with water, boulders as big as houses tumbling down the river, but this picture can be conjured. It
just takes a fair amount of staring at the bone-dry, stone-
dry cliff.

And so I stare for a while, not completely successful
at imagining Dry Falls wet, the canyon in front of me
filled with water, splashing over my feet. But I try.

The story of the Missoula Floods begins with the geologic episodes that formed the Pacific Northwest. Thirty-

seven million years ago, the Juan de Fuca plate, one of the earth's tectonic plates, was shoved under the edge of the North American continent, resulting in the Cascade Range of volcanic mountains. Between twelve and seventeen million years ago, the volcanoes—both stratovolcanoes and fissure volcanoes—erupted, and each eruption spread thick basalt over the Columbia Plateau. The compelling nature of this story is in the layers of fire and water.

As the millennia progressed, life and land flourished. Ice ages came and went. Species appeared and disappeared. Then, in the last two million years, the glaciers shaped the texture of the landscape as we know it. Volcanic activity laid down the raw materials, and the glaciers shaped it. Clay and hands, so to speak.

Then, action of a different sort: between ten and fifteen thousand years ago, during the last ice age, a finger of the Cordilleran ice sheet from Canada moved down and dammed up the Clark Fork River in northern Idaho. This created Glacial Lake Missoula, which flooded out most of western Montana. It's important to be accurate about this: the Missoula Floods were not a single event but happened repeatedly about every 50 years for at least 2,500 years. The ice dam would break and reform; the water would build up until the pressure broke the dam again. The ice dam was an estimated 2,000 feet high, creating a lake that was 200 miles long, 2,000 feet deep, and contained more water than Lakes Erie and Ontario combined. More than 500 cubic miles of water. When the dam broke, all that water went straight to the Pacific. A mountain of water.

The ice dam would have made noises. Creaking. Groaning. Cracking. Popping. All kinds of noises that humans attribute to ice. When the ice broke, it probably exploded into brilliant shards from the force of the water. The water, suddenly free, rushed toward the Pacific at ten times the combined flow of all the rivers in the world, shooting downriver at a speed of sixty-five miles per hour. The lake would have drained in as little as forty-eight hours.

A lake the size of Erie and Ontario combined, draining in two days.

Deluge seems too weak a word for this new river. *Frantic,* too weak an adjective. The Glacial Lake Missoula website supported by the Montana Natural History Center states that "the maximum rate of flow was equal to 9.46 cubic miles per hour (386 million cubic feet per second). This rate is 60 times the flow of the Amazon River, the largest river in the world today." As the water flooded down the Columbia, the river's already established gorge was not large enough to handle all the water, so the water went elsewhere, spreading out over Washington State, still heading for the freedom of the Pacific, taking with it much of the topsoil—hundreds of feet of topsoil—and carving coulees into the basalt bedrock, tearing the landscape back down to the memories of the fire that created it in the first place. The topsoil was dumped downstream, in southern Washington and northern Oregon, which is why the farmland there is so rich. The water carried two-hundred-ton boulders downstream and deposited them in the middle of what is now flat farmland.

Stone is not the eternal act of strength I like to think it is. Water is much more powerful. Since stone is not uniform, but rather a composite of mineral crystals, water can find its way into those tiny spaces—and when the water freezes and thaws, expanding and retreating, the water can force the rock to break. Look at the Grand Canyon if you want an extreme example of the battle between water and stone; on a smaller scale, look at the potholes in the asphalt at the end of winter. Mount Rushmore has gone through many cycles of repair to keep the sculpture intact. Repairs were not enough to save the Old Man of the Mountain in New Hampshire, which fell in 2003. The hundred-ton boulders in what is currently known as the Channeled Scablands in Washington might have been impressive in their original, apparently constant location, but when the floods came through, they rode the water from Montana just like everything else.

The beginning of Jonathan Johnson's poem "The Last Great Flood" describes the scene:

> *Two-thousand-feet of blue ice dam crumbled*
> *and slid into twenty-thousand-years ago,*
> *probably in the spring, in the warmth*
> *of an unnamed, sunny afternoon, or perhaps,*
> *after a sustained, heavy rain, with ten times*
> *the current of all the rivers in the world.*
> *Spontaneous overflow with no people,*
> *with no hazy empathy. Snapping larch*
> *and drowning herons, sure, but no awe.*
> *No imagination. No Red Cross. No vanishing point.*
> *Just westbound water spilling over this valley,*
> *down over Westmond and Cocolalla Creeks, widening*
> *across the Rathdrum Prairie, hellbent for the Pacific.*

Hellbent. Yes, hellbent.

Let's keep following the hellbent water through eastern Washington, from Spokane to Dry Falls, a drive that takes about two hours by car, give or take, because the next layer of the story is below the water. Picture the bottom of any lake, or even a riverbed: water, back and forth, back and forth—this action creates relatively uniform ripple marks. The same thing happened with Washington as a result of the Missoula Floods, but you would never connect the hills as being ripple marks unless you could see them from above—and the Missoula Floods ripple marks are visible from space. On the surface, what you see as you drive west from Spokane on Highway 2 is green farmland in the growing months and gorgeous gold in the harvest. The land is flat enough that you can see dust devils spinning in the distance, but the hills are thirty feet tall, and the land—which still strikes me as flat—is occasionally punctuated by immense boulders, with no real explanation as to how they got there. The boulders are tangible questions. Curiosity strikers. How can you look at something like that and not wonder, *How did they get there?* They are words made of stone, stones that tell the story of the Missoula Floods.

The story of the Missoula Floods does not stop after the creation of the Channeled Scablands, Dry Falls, or even Grand Coulee. The water dispersed as it flowed south with the Columbia, but not enough. The floods produced enough water to cover the land for weeks, maybe even months. The problem was the Wallula Gap, a place-name that rolls nicely off the tongue. *Wallula.* Bottleneck. The Wallula Gap prevented the water from moving down the Columbia to the Pacific. According to the USGS website, "For several weeks, as much as 200 cubic miles of water per day were delivered to a gap that could discharge less than 40 cubic miles a day." That's a very large traffic jam, especially if some boulders got stuck and plugged up the already small gap. I can imagine that—so clearly that I am surprised by the detail of my imagination. Geologists have speculated that the bottleneck created several very large temporary lakes, lakes that could have been as deep as 1,200 feet and covered 3,500 square miles. Evidence of how the lake formed is visible in the form of the hillsides, which bear watermarks. In the Columbia Gorge itself, the waters were probably 800 feet deep, and they eventually carved the gorge deeper and wider, creating the still-wet waterfalls along the river.

Usually whenever I traveled from my homeland of Minnesota to Spokane, I went by car, so it wasn't until two years after moving from Spokane that I saw the place from the air, en route from Ohio to Seattle. The pilot announced our final descent into SeaTac, and I looked up from my book, across the two people sitting between me and the window. Until that moment, I only knew intellectually that the ripple marks were visible from the air, and intellectual knowledge can only go so far. But as I tried to make out the landforms through the whispers of cirrus and stratus clouds, intellect became marrow. *The land really did look like ripple marks,* like the sand under the skin of the Minnesota lakes I am familiar with. For some reason, this surprised me. Sitting in my cramped airplane seat, I thought I could feel Washington squish between my toes, rasp against the tender arch of my foot where the skin is thin and vulnerable.

In these moments I feel that questions I haven't asked have been answered: the knowing is everything. The land does not respect thinking; it only respects the knowing. I could carry all the numbers and facts of the Missoula Floods around in my head for years without them actually meaning anything. Only when I saw the ripple marks for myself from the air, felt the ripple marks under my skin and under the tires of my car did the Missoula Floods become an actual event that is recorded into the land itself, not just a geological phenomenon that makes geologists smile. This shifts my wonder from a geological interest to a linguistic interest. And it makes the linguist, the historian, the storyteller in me smile.

Driving over the ripple marks is an experience, but only if you know what you're driving over. Otherwise, you're just driving in hilly country, where the hills are strangely straight and of uniform size—and how interesting is that? This is not rolling hills country, but it is compelling nonetheless, and more so if you know the topography, *the writing of the place*. And geography, *the writing of the earth*. And the petrography—literally, *the writing of the stone*. Something is recorded, written, there in the land in some form—otherwise we wouldn't have given terms to these concepts. If something had not been written there in some form, we would have chosen different words, ones that did not include *write*. There is a language here, but it isn't any language I can understand—which doesn't make it bad or nonexistent.

Petrography is defined as "description and classification of rocks," but I want to think of the word in terms of its literal translation: rock and writing. Stories in stones is not a new idea—and I'm not talking about carving human stories into stones. Stories carved into stones would be *petroglyphs* (and by extension, *hieroglyphics*), and while these human stories have their place, I'm talking about stories told when there was only land and sky, water and stone. I want to go back beyond creation myths, because they are still too human. I want to explore languages that are not audible, words made of stone. The idea is intriguing. What if you could walk along the glaciated valleys of the eastern Cascades, near Chelan, Washington, and read the petrography of the place? Would you be able to read the story of glaciers forming, moving down the valley, carving the V-shape of the valley into a U-shape? What would that story look like? I would call it a thriller, the tension of waiting for the glacier to grind the mountain down as it moves closer to the Lake Chelan gorge. Will the glacier melt and retreat before it gets there? To what extent will the glacier change the landscape? Will the story be long reaching, like the way some books have changed the mental landscape? Or will it burn brightly and disappear into obscurity? This is petrography, figuring out the story when the glacier is gone and all that remains is the scar tissue on the mountains. But petrography only works if you pay attention and have the capacity to be curious about the differences between V-shaped valleys and U-shaped valleys and wonder why they are different.

Languages that are not audible, stories whose words are written in stone, expand the consciousness. Sometimes we are too bound by the confines of our skulls. Just because we can't hear or read the stories written in stone doesn't mean they don't exist. The Irish essayist Tim Robinson writes of the effect of history and memory on Irish place-names, how something that happened long ago is immortalized by the name given to the place. In "Listening to the Landscape," he writes, "Life, for a language, is continuous self-transcendence. Nevertheless, each language has its own core of native strength and sweetness, and perhaps in the case of the Irish this is to be identified with its immediacy to experience, and in particular with its closeness to the land." What if the core, the basis of language, is something tangible? Stories themselves can often be traced to something tangible—but what if a language is tangible as well? What if the core of a language is rock—granite, basalt, sandstone? What if language is "identified with its immediacy to experience"—something like the Missoula Floods—and "with its closeness to the land"? What if it is identified through the land itself? Robinson continues:

> But, letting ourselves be swept along with the huge generalization, it would mean that Irish is a language less dominated by the prestige of the book, less individualistic in its stance towards the absolute, less hospitable to analysis, than those neighbor languages which were the immediate sites of these cultural upheavals. And these upheavals, these floods of thought, not only left rich deposits in those languages, but swept much away that had come to be seen as obsolete and valueless, and which we now feel want of. ("Listening to the Landscape," in *Setting Foot on the Shores of Connemara*)

Floods of thought leaving rich deposits of language—or stripping the consciousness down to the bedrock, getting to the bottom of the ideas in eastern Washington. Depositing the rich topsoil of the thought processes from that place onto southern Washington and northern Oregon.

Humans create much of the meaning that places hold, but not all of it. The concept always goes back to the basic idea of a tree falling in the forest and wondering if it makes a sound if nobody is around to hear it.

Are there really stories if there are no humans around to understand them? Humans didn't create the ripple marks or the meaning behind them, but it is obvious that there is a story attached to the landscape. Not knowing the story doesn't diminish it. We can see that something massive happened here. We can question the presence of the boulders. We may be unable to decipher their significance, but their significance is not diminished because of our ignorance.

Here's what I'm going after: On the mountains that surround Missoula, Montana, there is a watermark. It is clear that there is a story here—where did this watermark come from?—and just because we can't read the story in the watermark doesn't mean the story can't be read by someone else. It just takes a different perspective, one that J. Harlen Bretz and Joseph T. Pardee, the geologists who proposed the Missoula Flood theory, had. Reading the petrography involves thinking outside the box. The story here is that the watermark is the result of the present-day city of Missoula being under 950 feet of water during the flood years. The importance here is larger than human mortality, than oral history, than recognition of nonhuman stories. The importance of reading the petrography—or recognizing that the petrography exists—centers around consciousness and awareness. The importance of paying attention.

I grew up in the middle of Lakes Country, a hundred miles east of the Red River of the North, the border between Minnesota and North Dakota. This is topographically a different world from the prairie of western Minnesota where I currently live. There are ninety lakes in the ten-mile radius around my hometown. Driving north from my various childhood homes in Hubbard County to Bemidji, piles of boulders punctuate the farmer's fields. *Where did the rocks come from, Mom?* This question was standard on the trips to Bemidji—every trip, I would ask. I don't know if I forgot what she had said the time before or if I just wanted to hear it again—I tend to believe it is the latter. The boulders were brought down by the glaciers and left there when the glaciers receded and melted. The farmers moved the rocks into nice, neat piles so they could farm the land. Beyond that, geologic history has no visible presence where I grew up. The petrography is not obvious. Ripple marks are visible in the shallows of the lakes, but we don't pay them much attention, though they are a unique, pleasant sensation underneath bare feet.

There is a more logical link between Minnesota and the Missoula Floods and their effects on Washington beyond the obvious presence of water. Water is secondary— for once, I am not interested in the water. I'm interested in what is underneath and what is left behind. I'm interested in what is left on the surface, what happens after the evaporation, when the causes are all but forgotten and all that remains is the effect.

It is not what is there but what is missing that leads us a few hundred miles north of Hubbard County, to Rainy River and Rainy Lake, which form much of the border between Minnesota and Canada. One week during my college summers as a camp counselor, I led a group of houseboaters into Ontario, to Church Island in Rainy Lake, one of thousands of wooded islands in the Lake. I have lived around lakes all my life—I'm not easily impressed by them anymore—but Rainy Lake was different. Maybe because of the rock. This is what I am betting on.

Rainy Lake and its surrounds represent the southern area of the Canadian Shield, which contains some of the oldest exposed rock formations in the world. Here we have the beginning. The bedrock. The point from which zero is counted. Since the last glaciers moved through, soil has accumulated on most of Rainy's islands, allowing them to support trees as well as small plants and animals. The lake bed is rock, not soil. And since there is no soil, there is little in the water to support vegetation, which makes the water very clear. On the houseboat trip, we swam off the little point on the island, and though we always wore water shoes or sandals in the water, I wanted to feel the rock underneath my feet. Under my fingers it felt faintly rough, never slippery or slimy with algae or the other aquatic plants I was used to around home.

I often sat on the point when I had a few minutes to myself, on an extension of the rocks that led down into the water. I saw turtles sunning themselves on sunken logs, as well as bald eagles nesting in a dead tree. Pine trees, blue water, bald eagles, mating loons, hundreds of small islands. But I always returned, mentally, to the rock. This is one place where everything is exposed—and that exposure wasn't unnatural or jarring or any other Puritan adjective we might associate with *naked*. The naked Scablands in Washington strike me as unnatural. Covering the rock of Rainy Lake would be unnatural.

A friend and I once had a conversation about the geology of Minnesota and Washington; both of us were familiar with both places. The geology of Washington is right there in your face. On the surface, no pretensions. What you see is what you get. The bedrock of Minnesota is much deeper—sometimes as deep as a couple hundred feet. We Scandinavians like it that way. It's not that I think geography or topography molds our values and perceptions, but it is possible that it may reflect something of that sort. Of course this doesn't always fit. There is a contrast here between natural and unnatural exposure, of some kind of Puritanism when it comes to covering up the bedrock and the stories written there. I am not completely sure what significance it holds.

There is a contradiction here that is not exactly mutually exclusive, one that requires an active mental pursuit. The Washington petrography tells the story of the Missoula Floods. The Rainy Lake–Canadian Shield petrography is relatively absent of such words, to the point where I am not exactly sure of the story it holds. In Washington, the water is gone. On Rainy Lake, the water still laps the shore. Both places are stripped to the bedrock. One story is obvious. The other is not. There will never be ripple marks on the bed of Rainy Lake. How can the stories make their impression in something that will not yield, even after millions of years? The Washington bedrock was carved in a relatively short time. The bedrock of Rainy Lake is still relatively intact. How will we know what transpired to create the land of the Canadian Shield if we cannot read the text? What is the Rosetta Stone we can use to read the bedrock of Rainy Lake?

The simplest answer is that we may never be able to read the bedrock. The more complex answer is that the words are there if we know where to look. There is a story about how the bedrock came to be created. How it was stripped by glaciers. There is a story about the solid bed of the lake, the clarity of the water. There is a story about how the islands found their topsoil and were able to support vegetation. The words to the stories are there. I am convinced of it. I would be very disappointed otherwise.

On my desk sits a smooth, elliptical granite stone. I often find it on the floor, as my cat likes to bat it off my desk during the night. It's a perfect fit for my hand. I found it on Inishmore, the largest of the Aran Islands, back in 2000. Of all the souvenirs I brought back from Ireland, this stone is one of my favorites. Every time I handle it, I like to consider the most clichéd of petrographical questions: what was the petrography of this stone? It had come from somewhere, perhaps broken off the Inishmore cliffs, which had, in turn, broken off mainland Ireland, which had probably been connected to England and Scotland at one time and before that the Continent. Maybe it had come from somewhere else, somewhere farther away—how was I to know? After all of that, it was tossed around the sea and against other objects long enough to become perfectly elliptical, perfectly smooth. What had this rock seen in the span of that much time? What stories did it hold? What does it still hold, even as I hold the stone in my hand and wrap my fingers around it? Archaeologists and geologists and people who know what they are looking for can read the petrography—I do not number myself among them. I lean toward imagination, which may or may not be accurate.

The bedrock of the Aran Islands is exposed, like eastern Washington and Rainy Lake. The Arans share their geology with County Clare, which is a peculiar thing called *karst*—this area is known as the Burren. Like Rainy Lake and the Missoula floodplain, the Burren is shaped by water. Deep fissures slice up the limestone, trickles of the prevalent Irish winter rains culminate in something strong enough to dissolve the bedrock. The land is surface limestone—they say about the Burren that there isn't enough water to drown a man nor trees to hang him nor dirt to bury him. It is a strange landscape that only seems barren on first glance. But the Burren is home to more than the rare alpine plants that grow in the fissures.

This is petrography in its most real state. If it weren't for the words left in the stones, we wouldn't have the signpost to look for the stories. How else are we to know what we should, if there is no indicator? How are we to know what transpired in eastern Washington, on Rainy Lake, on the Burren if the story isn't written there somehow? This is the difference between the ripple marks and Rainy Lake. We can see the story of the Missoula Floods and its tributary stories written onto the landscape of the Pacific Northwest.

In Australia, the link between natural history and cultural memory is as pervasive among the Aborigines as air. Bruce Chatwin, in *The Songlines,* describes how "each totemic ancestor, while travelling through the country, was thought to have scattered a trail of words and musical notes along the line of his footprints, and how these Dreaming-tracks lay over the land as 'ways' of communication between the most far-flung tribes." Imagine the petrography of a place not being hidden. There is, of course, the lingering effects of creation myths and human influence in this scenario, because the stories recorded in the stones relate to the Ancestors, but the Dreamtime is an active use of petrography. Chatwin continues, "In theory, at least, the whole of Australia could be read as a musical score. There was hardly a rock or creek in the country that could not or had not been sung. One should visualize the Songlines as a spaghetti of *Iliads* and *Odysseys,* writing this way and that, in which every 'episode' was readable in terms of geology." I may be looking for geological stories like the Missoula Floods or what may be written in the lake bed of Rainy Lake, but there is a certain allure to having the ancient stories of a people written in the rocks and sand and trees of a region. The humans did not create the rocks or the sand or the trees, and they did not write their own stories there; they simply read what is there. Their stories may be different from what I am looking for, but the concept seems to apply.

The water in eastern Washington is gone. The glaciers that carved up most of North America are gone. The water that slices the limestone in the West of Ireland is still carving its petrography. What will the ripple marks be a million years from now? Will we be able to read the petrography? Will we only be left with the questions?

Where did the rocks come from, Mom?

Recorded History

I. Mount St. Helens, 2004

As I sit here, Mount St. Helens is rumbling. In the past
week, the news has been full of reports of thousands of
small earthquakes and movement in the lava dome of the
volcano. It could erupt in a matter of days, they say. For
some reason, this news is very exciting.

I lived in Washington State for a time, but not near
the volcanic mountains of the western side. I lived on the
eastern side of the state where the worst we had to worry
about were memories of the ice age floods that tore apart
the landscape. This may explain my original fascination
with Mount St. Helens, Mount Adams, Mount Rainier,
Mount Hood, and the rest of the Cascades volcanoes.
Maybe it is a flatlander's pull, a granddaughter's fascination with the photographs her grandfather took of Mount
Rainier decades before, on the wall in his bedroom so
high above her head that she can look up but never reach
them, but I don't think that is a full-enough explanation.

Part of it comes down to this: something happened

to change the physical and mental landscape, and I was alive when that happened. I could name others—but Mount St. Helens sticks. To be fair, I was not old enough to remember the eruption in 1980, but it is enough that I was a part of the before and after, even if the eruption did not specifically impact me. This may be a fundamentally selfish viewpoint, a flimsy reason for wanting to see Mount St. Helens erupt, to make an impression on my own memoryscape, but it is nonetheless there. I really wanted to know how the mental landscape would change as the physical landscape suffered. I wanted to know what would be said about this eruption, how it would be compared to the 1980 eruption, how it would be compared to other volcanoes. I wanted to rub the ash between my fingers, press the pumice into my palm, see if the synthetic glass obsidian created out of the 2004 ash would be as beautiful as that original 1980 helenite. What would it be like to wear a volcano on your hand, around your neck, catching the light and fracturing it just like the eruption did to the mountain? I wanted to see the scars on the mountain, I wanted to see how those scars healed, and if the new would be stronger than the old. I wanted to see it with my own eyes, feel the effects with my hands, my feet. I wanted to *know*.

Before Mount St. Helens blew in May 1980, little earthquakes in the two months leading up to the big blast had weakened the mountain. The north side started to bulge. A 5.1 earthquake on May 18 directly underneath the mountain triggered the largest landslide in recorded history: 23 square miles—0.67 cubic miles—of rock and debris obeyed gravity and took out everything in its path at a speed from 110 to 155 miles per hour. The landslide changed the pressure inside the mountain: instead of the volcano blowing up, it blew out its side because there was much less matter to block the volcano's path to fresh air on that north side. But the landslide was where I started, the place I kept coming back to—*the largest landslide ever?* In all of recorded history, this was the biggest? I couldn't immediately comprehend that, so I put the idea in my pocket for a while and went back to the numbers.

The lateral blast took out enough trees, according to the USGS website, to build 300,000 two-bedroom homes.

The pyroclastic flow—the volcanic gases, ash, and pumice—started moving at 220 miles per hour and accelerated to 670 miles per hour; it may have passed the speed of sound. The temperature of the spew was about 660°F, which melted the snow and glaciers on the mountain, adding torrents of water to the landslide and the pyroclastic flow. I learned that this combination of pyroclastic flow and water is called *lahar*.

If that wasn't enough destruction, the mountain then blew out its top, sending 490 tons of ash—0.26 cubic miles—fifteen miles into the air. The prevailing winds carried this ash as far east as the Dakotas and Minnesota, and as many as 57,000 square miles of the western United States were covered—or at least dusted—by ash. The ash circled the world in fifteen days. The energy released, according to the USGS website, was 24 megatons of thermal energy—thousands of times stronger than the Hiroshima A-bomb.

Before the eruption, Mount St. Helens was the fifth-tallest mountain in the lower forty-eight states. She lost 1,314 feet in the blast, sending her ranking down to about the thirtieth.

On October 1, 2004, Mount St. Helens burped, which was as close as she came to erupting, and rumbles in later years have not brought her any closer. I tried not to be disappointed that I couldn't live out my natural disasters vicariously, from the safety of my midwestern living room. Natural violence is fascinating because it is horrifying, beyond any sort of human control. There is a vulnerability that I appreciate, even as I know the absolute suffering such disasters cause.

I have gone over these numbers many times, returning to them, turning them over in my mind like tumbling stones. But in the end, they are just numbers, and I cannot make them stick to anything. Maybe my inability to wrap my brain around the Mount St. Helens blast is a result of a too-human failing: we seem to dismiss—or at least are unable to comprehend—numbers over ten, numbers that are beyond our ability to count on our fingers, or on the outside twenty—if we count our toes. Childishness aside, our fingers are a tangible way to count. We can see them. We can feel them. Numbers beyond the number of our fingers are always impressive because we don't really have a way to connect physically with numbers that large. We don't have a way to understand the world around us. And to understand the world is the whole point of keeping track of anything.

We measure numbers against what we know. My understanding of tall is measured by my own height of five-eight and my father's height of six-five. It is all about measuring what we do not know against what we do know. I know what six-five looks like, and everything I see is measured against that. If I want to really understand what the numbers of Mount St. Helens mean, especially the height loss, I have to look at photographs, before and after. Once, during my *Titanic*-obsession phase, I saw a drawing comparing the *Titanic* to other monuments of the time—the

Empire State Building, the Washington Monument, the Giza Pyramids. It's the same concept—proportional comparisons and perspective. This is what matters.

Beyond that, I really have no way of knowing, and the truth is that I don't really care, simply because no meaning is attached to that knowledge. I don't care exactly how many feet tall Mount Everest is—they tell me it is the tallest, and that is enough. The numbers game is merely a game of memory—pulling up specific numbers on demand. In *The Night Country,* Loren Eiseley wrote, "The effect does not lie in the height of the mountain. It does not lie in the scientific or descriptive efforts made on the way up. Instead the cumulative effect is compounded of two things: a style so appropriate to the occasion that it evokes the shape of the earth before man's hand had fallen upon it and, second, a terrible and original question posed on the mountain's summit." The effect of Mount St. Helens, then, would lie in the before and after. The shape of the earth before man's hand—or the land's own agenda—had affected it. And a "terrible and original question." What the shape of the earth was no longer applied. The terrible and *un*original questions could only be, *What now? Where to, from here?* The original answers would have to be something along the lines of what still remains. *What remains, amid all this destruction, that will tell the story of what happened?*

What recorded history comes down to is perspective, what is recorded in the land, the stories to be read when the lava and ash has cooled; what remains when the flowers and trees and deer and bear have returned to the slopes, and it looks like nothing ever happened in that place except sunshine and beauty. Mount St. Helens has erupted before, many times, and she will continue to do so. The story of her history is written there in her rock if we know how to read it. These Mount St. Helens numbers—the cubic miles of rock that constituted the largest landslide in recorded history, the temperature of the pyroclastic flow—these numbers are something to push against, something against which to measure how far we have come. Or not.

II. Recorded History

The state with the most volcanic activity is not Hawaii, but Alaska. Though South America and Indonesia have larger numbers of stratovolcanoes—volcanoes composed of layers of lava and ash—Alaska has, proportionally, the most stratovolcanoes in the world.

In 1912 Alaska's Mount Katmai erupted. Its subsequent collapse was a direct result of the formation of the new volcano Novarupta. This eruption was the largest of the twentieth century, with more than 7 cubic miles of ash deposited. Pyroclastic flows didn't stop for fifteen miles and settled 700 feet deep in some places. It was ten times more powerful than Mount St. Helens in 1980, but this one didn't affect human sensibilities much because it was so far away from civilization. The high-latitude location of the volcano also meant that the eruption—and the ash thrown into the atmosphere—did not impact the global climate the way more centrally located eruptions have done. Houses were not destroyed; people were not put into danger. The landscape was changed, obviously, but there weren't many people around to marvel at it.

III. Recorded History

The eruption of Mount Laki in Iceland in 1783 was the largest output of lava in recorded history. Benjamin

Franklin theorized that this eruption was to blame for cooler temperatures in ensuing months.

IV. The Way History Is Recorded

A series of four eight-by-ten photographs hang in a diamond pattern on the lakeside wall of my grandparents' cabin in northern Minnesota. The bedroom is small, with windows too tiny to do justice to the view outside. For the last several years of my grandfather's life, my grandmother slept in this bedroom, he in the other bedroom, so his Parkinson's symptoms would not keep her awake. But his body was not always fragile. When these photographs were taken, he had not yet been diagnosed with leukemia or Parkinson's, he still had the knees he was born with, and his aorta was still fifty years away from weakening into two aneurysms that almost, but did not, kill him. Even with the potential for heartache inside him that we knew nothing about, he remained a beautiful fixture in our lives, soft-spoken and wise, with a twinkle in his eye like sunshine. Never once did I see him get angry or lose his temper; just disappointing him was enough to dissuade the worst misbehavior.

I saw Rainier through the clarity of his lens, then through my own lens so many decades later, when I lived in Spokane and learned about how the city of Seattle is constructed, how its lovely mountains hold the promise of destruction, just like Vesuvius did for Pompeii and Herculaneum.

Rainier hasn't erupted in over a hundred years, and this worries the experts, because the longer a volcano goes between eruptions, the higher the likelihood that the blast, when it happens, will be cataclysmic. Rainier seems to have a major eruption every thousand years or so—and the last big one was around AD 1100. Those in western Washington have Mount St. Helens to use as a reference point, and they fear that Rainier will be much, much worse.

Volcanologists know that the glaciers and snow on the top of Rainier will melt, and they have projected the path of all the water: those projections take the deluge through downtown Seattle. The lahar, the muddy mixture of pyroclastic flow and the melted glaciers, will take out most of Seattle. The eruption itself is less predictable—the heat and ash in the air, the pumice falling like hail. Add each of those elements to the facts that the Seattle area is densely populated and that there are few exits to the city—and what remains is a very dangerous situation.

They say the same thing about when Vesuvius blows again. The way that history was recorded in Pompeii and Herculaneum in AD 79 may seem morbid and graphic, but it is the recording itself that is important. According to the book by Tom Simkin and Lee Siebert:

> This region is marked by traditions of record-keeping that go back thousands of years and by generations of historians devoted to mining those records. It is often called "The Cradle of Western Civilization," but it is also very much the cradle of volcanology. The earliest known documentation of volcanism is an Anatolian wall painting of a nearby cinder cone eruption about 6200 BC; the vigorous record of Etna goes back to 1500 BC; and the catastrophic eruption of Vesuvius in 79 AD, with the burial of Pompeii, continues to serve today as an object lesson in volcanism. The region has given us the first documented "new mountain,"

Monte Nuovo [Campi Flegrei], in 1538, the first "new island" at Santorini [Greece], in 197 BC, and the word "volcano" itself (derived from Vulcan, the Roman god of fire). *(Volcanoes of the World)*

This is vital to keep in mind when thinking about *what* was recorded in Pompeii and Herculaneum and *how* it was recorded.

In Pompeii, history was recorded in relief, in the negative. It was not what remained that was important but what did not remain. All living creatures in the area, human and animal, were disintegrated by the heat of the pyroclastic flow and the depth of ash and pumice dumped on the area. Only when the cities were rediscovered in the sixteenth century and scientists in the eighteenth century began to study the ruins did anyone realize that the lack of human remains at Pompeii did not indicate that the inhabitants had safely evacuated. Only then did they consider where everybody had gone: they had gone nowhere. Scientists poured chalk and plaster material into the voids in the pumice, and the casts revealed how many people had actually died in Pompeii: 3,500 of them, most in terrible, horrific, unimaginable agony. The story recorded at Pompeii could be read in three dimensions, in a way we could actually understand in a physical way. The story that was Pompeii did not have a happy ending.

At Herculaneum, along the Mediterranean shoreline, scientists also theorized about the lack of human remains and concluded that since Herculaneum was farther away from Vesuvius and did not receive the same deluge of ash and pumice that Pompeii did, the inhabitants of Herculaneum were able to escape. By sea, they thought—hoped, prayed, as no one wanted to entertain the thought that escape was impossible. But recently, they have discovered they were wrong; the prayers for mercy for those long dead went unanswered. In arched chambers along the shoreline, hundreds of skeletons have been found— men, women, children. The story recorded is that Herculaneum was destroyed in a different way than Pompeii. The people had time to get to the shoreline, possibly intending to get away by boat as was originally theorized. Did the pyroclastic flow or did the lahar overtake them before they could escape? The relaxed poses of the skeletons indicate that they did not choke or suffocate to death. Most likely, they died instantly from the intense temperatures of the pyroclastic flow.

The structures where they sought shelter faced the sea, not Vesuvius. Something prevented them from escaping, and they died there. Whatever that was is not recorded. The study of recorded history is about more than deciphering the obvious. It is about more than what is on the surface—or *not* on the surface. The study of recorded history is about paying attention, about wondering about causes and effects that cannot be measured on our fingers. It is about finding out what has really been recorded in the empty space between what is there and what is not there. The absence of a story is sometimes a story in itself.

V. The Way History Is Recorded

I sit in a barrel-vaulted room that reminds me of a rib cage; I am staring directly at a painting of a mammoth herd crashing through one of the rivers on the Great Plains of Nebraska. The lead mammoth, a bull, I assume, stares directly at me, the wrinkles of his trunk and the bags under his eyes, topped by a toupee of hair, remind me of an old man, a characterization that may explain why we think of his pachyderm descendants as wise. Voices of excited children echo off the walls, as if this chamber were designed to bounce voices and laughter off the bones of the long-dead giant mammoths and mastodons.

In this room there are ten skeletons of mammoths and mastodons that once roamed the place where I now sit. Next to tusks longer than my leg, mammoth and mastodon teeth resemble trilobites. These skeletons, with no lips to enclose their mouths, look like they are grinning. The children touch everything they are allowed to, as if they best understand the world through their skin, their fingertips, the palm of their hands. Touch—the skin itself—is the body's largest sensory organ, after all, something that these mammoths and mastodons had plenty of—surface area—to tell them about the world around them and what it all means.

To my right, in the next chamber, is an exhibit of the Bruneau-Jarbidge event, twelve million years ago, which created the Ashfall Fossil Beds. On the volcano explosivity index, the Bruneau-Jarbidge event in southern Idaho was a 6, large enough to wreak significant damage over a sizable area—an area that included the Great Plains where I am now.

I lose myself in the bones of five species of prehistoric horses, three species of prehistoric camels, the bones of rhinoceroses—one skeleton was found nose-to-nose with its calf. There are bones of smaller mammals that were the ancestors of the antelope and deer of the Plains, birds, and turtles and tortoises and other reptiles that largely remain the same today as they were then.

What makes the bones of the Ashfall Fossil Beds unique is that the matrix holds them in the same position as at their moment of death. The matrix, in paleontological terms, is what surrounds a fossil, the rock that encases it. What the matrix is constructed of can vary, from sandstone to basalt to volcanic mud to amber. A matrix holds the fossil in place, suspended. The fossil floats. It is a part of the land, yet it is not. It is of the earth, but not. It is uncovered, revealed.

The animals died standing up; they were fossilized in three dimensions—their bones did not collapse into two dimensions when the connective tissue disappeared. Most fossils collapse once the skeletons have been stripped of flesh by the scavengers who take advantage of the opportunity. There is nothing left to hold the bones together. If they collapse in a way that keeps the order of bones intact, we say that the skeleton is articulated. What a lovely description, as if the order of the bones allows us to speak of them. What is missing when we cannot articulate the bones?

In Kim Barnes's essay "The Ashes of August," published in *Forged in Fire,* we are taught the language of Idaho, the language of wildfires. Even on the first page, we get a spectacular grounding in light and color and taste (which is bookended in the last paragraph by a wonderful evocation of smell) and are told, "The riverbanks are bedded in basalt." It means something to know that your bedrock is basalt. It means something to know that Barnes's canyon was formed by volcanoes, as that one word tells us that this is a volatile place, formed by fire, from its earliest days. Since the essay itself is about wildfires that come every August, it means something to know that fire still forms the people who live here and answers the question, *What does it mean to live here, today?*

The answer is, *This is how we are connected.* A volcano

in Idaho twelve million years ago connects those of us who stand on the Great Plains to those who stand in Idaho, and it does not matter if we stand on flat or mountain, water or clay, because the mud that cakes our shoes in Nebraska can be traced directly back to a specific volcano in Idaho, to a specific moment in time, linked by science, by the glass shards of volcanic bubbles when they shattered.

VI. Recorded History

The largest volcanic eruption in recorded history was at Tambora, Indonesia, April 1815. There were 92,000 people killed: 10,000 from the direct eruption and 82,000 from the aftermath, starvation, and disease. A tsunami triggered by the eruption killed 3,600. Nearly two hundred years later, an earthquake in the same region triggered the largest tsunami without a volcanic eruption in recorded history and killed 275,000 people. The fact of an earthquake in this region in 2004 did not surprise me when I heard of it because this place has a history, and it is not written in flowers. Flowers die and disappear. What is written here is recorded in fire and water and blood. These are the inks that endure, the ones that time does not dilute. They tell the story of terrible upheaval, of death and pain, of bravery and survival, of love and sacrifice. Humanity cannot tell a story with voice that lasts so long. Eventually people die. Eventually pieces of a story are lost—or changed to make the story more interesting. What is recorded in the land, the remnants left behind by the volcanoes, cannot be changed. They may face the weather, which may file down some of the finer details, but the story itself cannot be changed or lost.

Tambora's eruption column was 28 miles high and

consisted of 36 cubic miles of ash and pumice deposited over 800 miles. (Mount St. Helens only tossed up 0.26 cubic miles of ash.) Whereas the Novarupta eruption a century later would not affect the world, Tambora's effect was larger than just a loss of life. The history recorded by Tambora was more widespread, not simply because of the eruption itself, but because the timing coincided with the Industrial Revolution and the first decades of new orders in France and the United States. The global climate change, already complicated by the Little Ice Age, owing to the eruption and the quantity of ash in the atmosphere, saw a lowering of the world's temperature by three degrees Celsius. Stories often have a way of changing our mental climates as well. The kind of thinking that would get humanity through life *before* the volcano would not be the same thinking that would get the world through the *after*.

Recorded history itself, the story of what happened at Tambora, would never change. The fact is that the world was not the same after Tambora; therefore, change would have to be registered in every field that could measure change, from science and climate to politics and literature. According to Brian Fagan, in *The Little Ice Age: How Climate Made History, 1300–1850,* the food shortages caused by the climate changes due to Tambora's eruption, the crop failures, and the threats of violence by starving peasants in places like France, which was still wary after the recent revolution, caused the governments of those places to take care of their poor in a way they never had before in times of economic crisis. In the United States, the federal government did almost nothing; the state of New York took the responsibility of creating the Erie Canal for the purpose of moving food to and from rural areas. Fagan writes, "These policies were the greatest legacy of the Tambora eruption." Europe and North America were learning to accept that their lives could be changed drastically by something so far away, something they had no control over. The mental shift might have been as painful as any other effect of Tambora. Even governments could not hold.

VII. The Way History Is Recorded

The story of a story starts with such things. While Tambora was greater than the 1450 BC eruption of Santorini, the destruction of Santorini is what gave rise to legends of Atlantis. Such catastrophic destruction could only have been the work of the gods, punishment for moral failings. These are the stories we tell to explain the unexplainable.

VIII. Eight

Volcanologists have established the volcanic explosivity index to rate the severity of volcanic explosions. It ranges from 0 (a nonexplosive eruption—like Kilauea on Hawaii, which has been erupting continuously since the 1980s) to 8, which has only happened twice. Mount St. Helens (1980) was a 5. Vesuvius (Italy, 79), was a 6, as was Krakatau (Indonesia, 1883), an earlier Mount St. Helens eruption (1855), and Mount Pinatubo (Phillipines, 1991). Tambora (1815) rated a 7.

Only two volcanoes are considered an 8 on the scale, but neither is in the realm of recorded history: the Yellowstone caldera eruption of 640,000 years ago and Mount Toba, on the island of Sumatra, 71,000 years ago. These may have preceded human methods of recording history, but what the volcanoes left behind was a recording of their own, and it is necessary to read between the lines to figure out what was recorded. In recorded history, in human history, there has not been an eruption rated 8. I am grateful.

The Mount Toba eruption on the island of Sumatra 71,000 years ago blew 192 cubic miles of ash and debris into the air. I try to compare the devastation caused by Mount St. Helens's puny cubic quarter-mile with almost two hundred cubic miles, but I fail. I cannot picture it. So I find numbers I can comprehend, proportional, perspective numbers. Seventy-five percent of northern hemisphere plants died, followed by a thousand-year-long ice age, which only a few thousand people survived. What remained was recorded in that way—another example of history being recorded in the negative. Fossils are often imprinted in the negative, after all. And the way they survive tells us the story left behind.

The volcanic explosivity index gives us something to push against—numbers provide us the perspective we are looking for. Height, temperature, speed, energy released, volume of ash and debris. It is not enough to study a volcano and think, *Oh, that was a biggie*—we need to compare it to other volcanoes. And I mean *need* quite specifically. How else can we record our own personal, human growth—personal and communal? Humanity is about *more*: the next hurdle, the next day, the next personal milestone. But how can we measure *next* when we do not know where we stand at *this* moment?

IX. The Way History Is Recorded

As much as I would like some things to fade into the neverland of forgotten memory, the fact that I write things down in my commonplace books prevents this from happening—and this is the whole point: memory solidified into something to be comprehended by those who come after. Max W. Thomas writes, "Commonplace books are about memory, which takes both material and immaterial form; the commonplace book is a record of what that memory might look like." Commonplace books are a collection of brief thoughts, events, quotations; they are not as personal as a journal.

My first commonplace book, started when I was seventeen, is now one of four. Carefully flipping through its pages—the binding is broken—I realize that this book represents five years of my life. This surprises me a little. So much time contained in such a small space. The second book represents four years. The third book, nearly seven. I have written only two entries in the fourth.

As the years go by and the books fill up, I worry about how long they will last before the pages begin to fall out. Human history—and the time before recorded history—is rarely saved on something as fragile and temporary as paper. There is good reason for this. With the volcanoes, the story of the planet is recorded in rock, in pumice, in what is contained between the petrified layers. But humans continue to value paper as the best medium to record their own history. We gave up carving rock thousands of years ago—what have we forgotten since then?

Sometimes, because recorded history is not in a form or language we recognize, we sometimes think it is not there. If we are lucky, we are led to try harder to read between the historical lines, to look at how history may be recorded in relief, like Pompeii, to understand the history of a region like Indonesia, so that we are not terribly surprised when activity—like the 2004 tsunami—happens there, and so we can understand why that region is prone to such things.

The purpose of such an exploration is to unlock our link to peoples and times and events before us—because history does repeat itself. The purpose is to avoid being caught unaware, if possible. The purpose is to break out of our self-centered world, to see how the physical world itself impacts the self, even indirectly, even from thousands of miles away. The purpose is to think outside the box and understand that there is a direct relation between animal, vegetable, and mineral that the animal cannot control. The purpose of exploring the history recorded by the volcanoes is to understand a cause-and-effect relationship between power and beauty, power and destruction, death and rebirth, cycles that need to find their full circumference for the world to be in balance. Volcanoes may destroy, but they also create. Understanding the history recorded in the volcanoes is one path to fully realizing the purpose of humans on a fragile and complex planet by way of what has come before, and then using that to understand what the future holds.

That is the whole point of having recorded history: not for the past, but for the future.

X. The Way History Is Recorded

Mount Tambora erupted more than a year ago. The temperatures are not summerlike and will not be for several years. The weather is poor enough to keep Mary Shelley, wife of Percy Bysshe Shelley, indoors. She is an educated woman, and her companions, her husband Percy and their friend Lord Byron, are men of letters, nobility who do not worry about suffering through poor harvests and crop failures. To them, the cold temperatures simply mean they cannot pursue what diversions they might have otherwise. Idleness does not suit them—at least mental idleness does not suit them. One of them proposes a contest: who can write the best ghost story? A fine challenge, since they are all stuck inside. Before long, Percy and Byron give up. After all, they are poets. Prose does not fit them well. Mary keeps going—she has nothing better to do. When she finished, the result was one of the most enduring horror tales of any generation.

Frankenstein is still with us; Tambora's influence is still with us, even though summers eventually returned to normal, and gradually time and distance erased the conditions and the reasons *Frankenstein* was written. But the mental landscape, the memoryscape, a tale of horror born of a tale of a horror, never returned to normal. *Frankenstein* would remember, even if no one else would.

XI. Krakatau, Indonesia, 1883

Krakatau was the first major volcanic eruption in the age of technology; its eruption and the aftermath was accessible to the entire world. Krakatau's eruption on August 27 and 28, 1883, was rated a 6, on par with Novarupta (1912) and Pinatubo (1991). Tom Simkin and Richard Fiske, in *Krakatau 1883: The Volcanic Eruption and Its Effects,* observe, "Only in southeast Sumatra did Krakatau itself claim victims, by its burning ash and red-hot pumice; elsewhere it was the waves that killed." Pumice, the rock that floats. The tsunamis, plural, wiped out 36,000 people and washed away 165 coastal villages. Fire and water did not cancel each other out. Nothing was of the natural order here. Nothing was understandable. Yet it had to be understood. There had to be some semblance of natural order somewhere.

These numbers came back to me in December 2004, when an earthquake hit the island of Sumatra, and the ensuing tsunamis killed an incomprehensible number of people. The numbers stunned me. The quake measured 9.1, the result of two of the earth's tectonic plates rubbing against each other. The tectonic activity that produced this quake is also why the volcanoes of this area are so active. The quake occurred about one hundred miles from Sumatra, the same region where Krakatau had thrown out a 6-magnitude eruption more than a hundred years before. The volatility of the geography makes this place what it is, and the volatility of the geological history is indelibly recorded in the land. The people of the area had to know it was only a matter of time before the volcanoes that formed their land returned to reform and reshape. Nothing changed just because humans moved in. The land has a longer memory than that.

Simkin and Fiske write in *Krakatau 1883,* "It is hard to overemphasize the fact that volcanic lifetimes are vastly longer than human memories." A hard-to-imagine thing, considering that the higher the death toll, the longer the memory. Future generations are left to piece together what happened and how it could have happened, given what remains: six-hundred-ton blocks of coral where they should not be. The steamer *Berouw* was washed well over a mile inland by one of the massive tsunamis that the eruption produced. The ship stayed in its location, relatively intact, for almost a hundred years after the eruption, but it was carved up for scrap in 1979. If it had stayed there, an explanation would have been required as human memories faded. The ship was tangible evidence that something had happened, even if no one remained to tell the story. *What happened here? How? Why? What do we do about it? Where do we go from here?*

Telegrams recorded what had happened, histories

recorded not in tangible terms but in wires and dots and dashes: telegrams received in Singapore from Batavia—which would later become Jakarta—one hundred miles from Krakatau. Here are some of the more startling excerpts:

> *Darkness covered the Sunda Straits from 10 am on the 27th until dawn the next day.*
>
> *Giant waves reached heights of 40 m above sea level, devastating everything in their path and hurling ashore coral blocks weighing as much as 600 tons.*
>
> *When the eruption ended, only 1/3 of Krakatau, formerly 5x9 km, remained above sea level, and new islands of steaming pumice and ash lay to the north where the sea had been 36 m deep.* (Simon and Fiske, *Krakatau 1883*)

Simkin and Fiske report that the veil created by the ash made the sun appear in shades of blue and green and created spectacular sunsets around the world. In New York City, Poughkeepsie, and New Haven, they report that fire engines were called to put out what were apparently fires—but were only vividly red sunsets.

Beauty and destruction, hope and fear, love and death. If we can figure out how to stack those building blocks, what will we know? What will we see when we stand on them? Even now, in November 2007, the volcano known as Anak Krakatau—Krakatau's Child—has been erupting. In the place where Krakatau used to be, a new volcano rose from the sea in the 1930s and has been growing ever since. If we could stand on its ever-expanding summit, what would we see?

XII. The Way History Is Recorded

The Year without Summer, 1816, was the direct result of Tambora blowing in April 1815. This was a terrible time in modern human history, a time already socially and politically fragile. Hundreds of thousands around the world starved because the cold temperatures killed crops. Because of the more central latitude of the eruption, the ash that Tambora tossed up affected more populated atmospheres and lowered the earth's temperatures by an average of 3°C. Crops died, people starved—from Southeast Asia to Europe and the Americas. No one was left unaffected, no one on any continent. Obviously humanity cannot be separated from their ecology, even if the ecology is not accessible or known.

And if Tambora, a 7 on the volcanic explosivity index, did that much damage ecologically, I wonder what the volcanoes rated at 8 did to the earth's temperature. It doesn't take an 8 eruption to change the climate. Tambora in 1815 and Pinatubo in 1991, just to name two, caused cooler temperatures across the globe. Pinatubo is a volcano of my lifetime, one I remember hearing on the news, though it did not impact me in a way I remember, mostly because the world of high school is so insulated. These days, I have a cousin who is in Manila, working on a master's degree, and she and her husband just had a baby girl. I hear news of mudslides and things—and I worry. Pinatubo is only sleeping.

But Pinatubo is something I can push against in order to try to imagine Tambora—and the effects that Tambora must have had. The area of northwest Ohio where I currently live was settled in the early 1810s and probably had as much to do with the establishment of communities around Fort Meigs and the end of the War of 1812 as with Tambora. The fact is that the preliminary taming of Ohio and the places that would become known as the Midwest made it easier for New England farmers to leave their farms after Tambora caused their crops to fail. Nothing would grow there. It was too cold. I come from farming families—I know the delicate balance between crop and climate. There was nothing delicate about the summer of 1816.

An 1892 article from the *Decatur County Journal* (Indiana) recalls the "year without summer." January and February were the spring months. March was cold, and winter arrived in April. Sleet and snow occurred nearly every night in June: "The snow was five inches deep for several days in succession in the interior of New York and from ten inches to three feet in Vermont and Maine." July saw ice, albeit thin—described as the thickness of a windowpane—but in August, the ice thickened to an inch, killing nearly every plant that had not already been killed. People couldn't stay. They would die if they stayed. And so Tambora caused the first mass migration out of New England into the Ohio Valley and beyond. History would be recorded onto new territory, with new pens and new paper, with new languages. Arguments can be made as to whether we would have reached this point in our own development and history without Tambora—I don't think we would have. We would have reacted to a different catalyst and gone in a different direction. What would our history look like, written only on the soil of New England, in the language of those early Americans, most of whom were of English origin? Without Tambora, people would not have left behind their land in Europe that only meant death, and the history of our country would not have been written in the richness of the Plains, in German and Swedish and Norwegian, history recorded in a land far away from the original volcano, but recorded nonetheless.

I am trying to imagine the early years of the fledgling democracy when things were already hard enough. We were trying to keep our independence from Britain; we were wary of what Napoleon was doing—and watching for how it would affect us. We were pushing our way into Indian Territories, stirring up new conflicts. We were just hoping for status quo, for things to be manageable enough for us to hold on and inch our way forward. And then a volcano—*a volcano*—thousands of miles away erupts.

We had written our desire for independence on paper once. Now we would write our independence on an entire continent. We would write our independence in footprints, with plows, with rifles. Writing history takes movement of the hand, gripping the pen and moving it across the paper. Recording history on land, whether by human hand or not, also takes movement. We may look to the recorded history of the past for what we can learn, but it only matters when it connects with our present to point the way to the future. The story of the volcanoes, what is recorded in their history is this: nothing stays the same. There may be periods of dormancy, but there is always a catalyst waiting under the surface, and it is written there, if we know how to pay attention. There are stories to be told in the movement, some good, some bad, but the lesson of the recorded history is that humanity cannot—or will not—stay in one place. It cannot ignore its surroundings if it hopes to survive.

So here I am, standing on the clay of the Great Black

Swamp in northwestern Ohio on a rainy and cold day, wondering what history is recorded here. I am left with one conclusion: everything I need to know about life I can find under my feet in this place. Past, present, and future are an elaborate musical chord, not separate notes. I know why it is flat. I know why it has the soil composition it does. I know why this land is such good farmland. I know why it floods the way it does, like it is doing right now. I know that Ohioans cannot exist separate from their recorded history, even though it is not written in lava and ash and pumice. I know that this land here is not the result of volcanoes, but it has been shaped by them—almost as much as it was shaped by glaciers and the retreating of Lake Erie. And somewhere in the recorded history of this soil remains the memory that brought people across it, brought the knowledge to drain the swamp so it could be farmed, and if we dig deep enough into the clay, the ink from the volcanoes will stain our hands black.

Holden

Ablation: refers to all processes by which snow, ice, or water in any form are lost from a glacier—the loss of snow or ice by evaporation and melting.

—U.S. Geological Survey

L ate June 2005. Trail to Hart Lake, Railroad Creek Valley, Holden Village, Wenatchee National Forest, Eastern Cascades, Chelan County, Washington. A four-and-a-half-mile hike, it is rugged enough that it's hard to judge how far we have walked. The sun is hot and high in the narrow strip of sky visible between the sides of the valley, the light and heat often filtered through the trees but not enough to lower the temperature.

We are surrounded by water, inside and outside. We carry three backpacks between the five of us, filled with the bare minimum required for this hike in this weather. We have a total of thirteen thirty-two-ounce bottles, each weighing about two pounds. Though essential and op-pressively heavy, this is not the kind of water we crave, even though we know that if we do not drink, if we do not sweat, we are in serious trouble. The temperature is in the nineties; it is natural that we wish for ice.

Ice carved the Railroad Creek Valley, 3,200 feet above sea level, glaciers that were, at one time, four thousand feet thick. We pause, lift our bottles, and drink the valley. Memories of the glaciers drip down our chins and evaporate before they land on our shoes, leaving behind a puff of glacial till dust—glacial flour, they call it—that sticks to our sunblock.

We laugh as we walk, our voices echoing off the valley walls, reflected back by the memory of the shiny minerals once mined from these mountains—copper, tin, gold—and on the bounce, the sound is caught in the curve of the J trees and held there. We will learn later that the tree trunks are bent in this curious J shape because the weight of the snow in the winter causes them to bend in their growth to accommodate it. We wonder what that weight would feel like and how long the trees resist before they surrender to the weight of the snow. Is it a burden or is it comforting? We feel our shape as a family bending on this trail, too. It isn't conscious, but when we look back, we can point to this trail and say, *This is where it happened,* even though we are not sure what *it* is.

Maybe this trail is the first time we carry our share of the weight rather than letting our father carry it all himself.

Maybe this is the first time that we have to wait for our parents to catch their breath, and we see in their faces a vulnerability we are not quite ready to face.

Maybe it is simply the first time that our parents look at us and see, rather than children, their equals.

Or maybe it is that we finally understand that the

bond we find ourselves forming will, at the end of the trail, be the result of choice, not obligation.

The ascent is gentle until we near the last rise, on the other side of which is Hart Lake. The rocks under our feet become more substantial, more than the dust we have been walking on for the last several hours. We must watch our step more closely, especially as we attempt the descent. Gravity seems especially strong here. We look up, but do not see a glacier. We look past the cirque that the glacier carved, down the valley, where we see the text of the glacier written on the stone, where the movement of ice has changed the language of the place from its original V shape to a U shape. We see its present, the melt that fills the valley. If we give a passing thought to the future of Hart Lake, it is fleeting. We sit down to rest and take off our shoes to soak our feet in the water, which is almost too cold to bear. We drink the water from our packs, and for a while, the five of us return to the children we once were in a splash of glacial melt that will evaporate from our hair and skin and clothes before we are ready to be dry.

While twilight settles outside, three hundred of us gather in the Village Center—the VC—for the vespers service. The wood of the VC warms, the paneling, the pews, the beams of the ceiling, and it seems to radiate more than heat. The cantors are young, with voices larger than they were. I know this music, known as *Vespers '86* inside Holden Village and *Holden Evening Prayer* outside it. Tonight, though, three hundred voices join, feeling the music, the richness of the notes, and the harmony in our blood.

There is an intimacy in singing the music of a place in its setting. Marty Haugen, a college classmate of my mother's, was seeing the same mountains, breathing the same air, feeling the same glory in his veins when he wrote this service in 1986. How could anyone look at those mountains, at the people around, and not wonder at the glory of creation? And not feel like shouting and hearing the echo off the mountains? Who is to say it was our own voices returning to us?

Is this the ultimate of what happens when the right words meet the right paper? When the right music meets the right ear? When the right temperature, the right temperament, the right temper combine? What does that landscape look like, inside and out? What does rightness look like? Does it look like a mountain, a glacier, a river? I don't know.

But I know what rightness sounds like.

Gretel Ehrlich, *The Future of Ice*:

> River sounds push Gary into sleep, and I listen to
> *sila*—how the mind-litter roils with chaotic weather.
> We are made of weather and our thoughts stream
> from the braid work of stillness and storms. For
> years Nietzsche searched for what he called "true
> climate," for its exact geographical location as it
> corresponds to the inner climate of the thinker.

Jonathan Johnson, from "Three Hours out of Fairbanks":

> to slip into the big story, glacier melt
> where words just forming

cave in and crumble to soil
in an un-named creek
that tightens its bend, the whole of sensation
now soluble, pulled downstream

I'm sitting here on the porch of Lodge Two, overlooking
a good portion of Holden Village, a former copper mine
village, home to a Lutheran retreat center since the early
1960s. It wasn't long before the village's mission included more than Lutherans and welcomed those of different
creeds and beliefs, advocating a mostly organic, mostly
locally sourced food system and practicing an environ-
mentally friendly approach to water and energy use. The
five of us, which includes my two younger sisters, take to
these tenets as if we had always lived this way.

The dining hall is at twelve o'clock; other lodges
occupy my peripheral vision. Beyond the physical buildings, we are surrounded by mountain peaks. I have been
in mountains before, but I have never been in a place like
this. I have never been so hemmed in by a landscape and
not felt claustrophobic, not felt the need to get out, get
to the top of the mountains. I'm sitting here, comfortable
in my jeans and sweatshirt, curled up in the chair with
my feet on the railing and my hands wrapped around
a mug of tea. It is early July, and while my own Minnesota is into triple-digit heat indexes, this high up in the
Cascades, it is not what I would term summer weather.
But the flowers here are blooming, purple and red and
orange and pink and yellow, so many colors that I don't
know the names of them all. The sky is blue; the mountains are green with trees.

The sunlight off the tailings is bright with discarded
copper and other minerals, the tailings that are slowly

poisoning Railroad Creek, which runs down the mountain to Lake Chelan. The mining company is liable for cleaning up the tailings, but it will be many years before the court battle is finished and work begins. In 1938, when the mine was operational, the tailing dike broke; the result was all the water between Lake Chelan and the mine was no longer safe. The state did nothing about it, breaking a promise to protect the water before mining interests. Now, the tailings must be dealt with, the riverbed scoured to remove contaminants, the land doused with lime to decrease its acid content, and more. The process will take years.

The eternal questions still arise: What is the inherent value of a place? Is it valuable only if money can be made from it, after it is no longer purely natural and becomes economic nature, political nature? What happens when no more money can be dug from it? Why is land so much more valuable than water; why is the Ogallala Aquifer less important than the land required to construct an oil pipeline over it from Alberta to the Gulf of Mexico? Where are economics and politics in that question?

Yesterday was so hot I wanted to be water. I was dissolving anyway, my body liquifying and hitting the dirt in little droplets, so I might as well be a puddle. I stood at the base of Ten Mile Falls, with two more miles to go to Monkey Bear Falls, and the water tumbling down the various levels of the falls, tripping over the trees that had fallen into the river, splashing around the rocks, looked like fun. The glacial melt was oxygen white, not turquoise green, and the sound it made as it foamed over those various obstacles of differing sizes and hardness sounded like a smile. It didn't sound like laughter—it was too much of a low-grade roar for that. Not enough bass rumbling to sound like laughter. The falls sounded like delight in its purest form. What about that wouldn't be fun? Had I not been human and endowed with so many nerve endings, I might have jumped in and tumbled down the river for the sheer joy of it.

But I am human.

While waiting for the boat to take us down Lake Chelan, back to our car and civilization, my sisters jumped off the dock and into the lake. The air temperature was comfortably warm, which contrasted strongly with the frigid temperature of the lake water. This is glacial melt, after all. The water is the most glorious blue-green color, a color reserved only for glacial lakes, a color my mother wants to suggest for crayon boxes, a color that is the result of the sediment carried by the glaciers. Even the sky, whether gray or true blue, does not change the color of the water. They splashed around, did some impressive dives, and bowed dramatically to applause when they found the dock again. They said it was actually better when they were here in the dead of winter and jumped in—there wasn't as much shock because of the lesser difference between air and water temperatures. I still thought they were crazy, but they were a part of this particular world in a way I would never be.

Faults

A 5.9 earthquake shakes the East Coast on August 24, 2011, toppling spires and cracking walls at the National Cathedral, agitating the confidence of people who had never recovered from the earth-shattering moments of 9/11. Californians sneered. But the last time the earth moved like that at the Pentagon, a plane had crashed into the outer rings of the building. On the East Coast, buildings shaking means something completely different from anywhere else in the world.

Charles Darwin writes, "A bad earthquake at once destroys our oldest associations: the earth, the very emblem of solidity, has moved beneath our feet like a thin crust over a fluid;—one second of time has created in the mind a strange idea of insecurity, which hours of reflection would not have produced" *(A Naturalist's Voyage round the World).*

But it is also nearly two hundred years since the New Madrid earthquakes caused the Mississippi River to run backward. They say that the New Madrid fault, the most active American seismic zone outside California, has a quake of that magnitude every two hundred years. The winter of 1811–12 was not unusual, in the large scheme of things. Right now, I am living in Nebraska, on the outer edge of the New Madrid fault zone. These things matter.

The Minnesota Scandinavians of my blood and acquaintance do not value such outward emotions. We are not effusive in affection, anger, or anything in between. The mythology of my Swedish-German blood would tell of a still-waters kind of people, not earthquake people, not hurricane people. But this is also my experience: My grandmother disapproved of clapping in church. I never heard my grandfather raise his voice, ever. We value subtlety. Our emotions are strong, but not often verbally expressed. When my grandfather died, I never saw my grandmother cry, but her grief was a real thing. We like the earth under our feet to be tilled, sown, fertilized, and harvested—this is something we can understand, filtered through "faith without works is dead." My grandfather showed his love for his family not in words but by returning to the farm to assist his brother with the work when his brother was injured. We like control. We do not think highly of those who cannot control themselves.

But I am envious of those who have experienced earthquakes. I do not want to live in California, but I want to feel the earth move under my feet. When the news reports seismic shivers where I happen to be living in Ohio or Nebraska, and I do not feel them, I feel cheated. I want to see granules of dirt shake and blur with power they have no control over. I want to stand in the middle of a field, away from buildings that might fall on me, and be moved. What would such an experience shake loose? What thoughts and emotions would be tossed around, and what would become of them? What would happen if I saw something as iconic and consistent as the Mississippi River flow backward, the Mississippi whose headwaters I have waded through more times than I can count, the headwaters that are so near my hometown? What would that look like in the context of a human life, one in the twenty-first century? What would happen after the river returned to its normal flow?

The danger here is the danger of all uncontrollable naturals: only the biggest are worthy of notice. The strongest earthquake, the most property damage, the highest death toll. This is dangerous because even little naturals can shake a foundation, move a person. I have never had my foundation seriously shaken, whether structural or emotional. On one hand, I am exceptionally grateful. On the other hand, I want something to shake my personal foundation so I can know for sure how sturdy my structures are. I want to know, not just believe, that what I hold dear will remain dear.

In five days, I will start observing the two-hundred-year anniversary of the New Madrid earthquakes, which began on December 16, 1811. Two earthquakes rustled northeastern Arkansas at a magnitude of at least 8.0, along the route of the New Madrid fault line. Two more earthquakes jostled Missouri on January 23 and February 7, 1812, both also rated higher than 8.0. There might have been a third earthquake in Arkansas that would have been above 8.0, which together would make five 8.0 or higher earthquakes in a two-month period. Six million square kilometers were damaged in some way. The area was sparsely populated, so casualties were slim and property damage was minimal, all things considered. But the area affected was two or three times larger than the

1964 Good Friday quake in Alaska and ten times the area affected by the 1906 San Francisco quake, according to the USGS website.

This section of the country prides itself on minding its own business. There is nothing in this landscape that would indicate that kind of volatility. It is mostly flat, mostly farmland. Certainly Tornado Alley makes things interesting, and the Dust Bowl was something nobody wants to repeat, but this is supposed to be solid, dependable land. We are supposed to be able to understand this land under our feet. So our next question becomes, *Was this an act of God?*

Natural disasters have been morality tales since the beginning of time. Plato's writings of Atlantis's destruction explain the disaster through the wickedness of the people. The same is true of the biblical flood. Who can forget Pat Robertson exhorting that the 2009 Haiti earthquake was the result of the Haitian pact with the devil, that God's wrath was to blame for Hurricane Katrina? While the majority of people took extreme offense at his ridiculousness, the premise is a very old one. When events happen that are beyond our comprehension, we reach for that which still encompasses everything we know and everything we do not and everything we cannot.

Theodore Steinberg, though, writes that considering natural disasters as acts of humans—that is, as scientifically and objectively understandable events—is fairly new. As we began to understand more about how the planet functions, we were less likely to explain disasters as acts of God. But the shift is larger than religion to science. This also marks the shift toward nature as political and economic. Steinberg's 1996 article "What Is a Natural Disaster?" in *Literature and Medicine* mentions the

1889 Johnstown flood, which complicates the definition of "natural disaster." It is true that spring rains contributed to the problem, but it was the collapse of the faulty dam that caused the disaster. The bulk of his article considers the cloud seeding and weather modification undertaken during the 1960s drought in the northeast, which seriously undermines the idea of what is a "natural" disaster. Similar things happened during the Dust Bowl, as desperation led people to do anything they could think of—however illogical it might seem—to end the drought. The point that Steinberg is trying to make is this: "Weather modification offended their moral sensibility by giving some people an upper hand with nature at the expense of others." As the ideas of acts of God versus acts of humans developed during this time, some blamed Hurricane Camille in 1969 on the effects of cloud seeding and weather modification. Steinberg quotes Paul Hoke, president of the Tri-State Natural Weather Association, "Since Congress appropriated the money for such cloud-seeding projects, [Hurricane] Agnes [in 1972] was more properly classified . . . not as an act of God, but an act of Congress."

Later in his article, Steinberg writes, "As the human will has more and more made its mark on the natural world, clear-cutting forests, altering the atmosphere, seeking to control earthquakes with underground drilling, and so forth, it has become increasingly difficult to discern the line between the natural and the cultural." Is there such a thing as an independent nature, he asks? He considers Bill McKibben, who argued, "It is no longer possible to think of nature as wholly independent from the activities of humankind."

On New Year's Eve 2011, a 4.0 earthquake struck north-eastern Ohio, the eleventh of such earthquakes in that region in the recent past. What is different about this earthquake—and the others related to it—is that it's our fault. The earthquake was caused not by fracking in the shale of northeastern Ohio but by the wells that disposed of the fracking fluids, which are a pressurized mixture of chemicals, sand, and water. Again, the questions come up: How do we define natural disaster? Do we consider the effects of mountaintop removal methods of coal mining natural disasters? How do we think about the arguments for and against the Keystone XL pipeline across the Ne-braska Sandhills and the Ogallala Aquifer, the same argu-ments for and against the Sandpiper pipeline across Hub-bard County, Minnesota, so close to the headwaters of the Mississippi? How do we continue to argue that uranium mining just outside the politically protected areas of the Grand Canyon should still be prohibited? What do we do about the power of money and influence to redraw the boundaries of the Ogalalla Aquifer, just so a man can put a nuclear waste dump in Texas and reap the benefits? Is it a natural disaster if people are not affected, property not destroyed? If the forest fires in Yellowstone in 1988 or the Boundary Waters in 2011 didn't hurt people, are they still disasters? After all, some species of plants require fire to germinate. The Great Plains requires fire to keep its ecology intact. How do we control natural disasters—and to what extent should we?

We can control the earthquakes caused by fracking—but will we? Should we? Where do we find the line of *enough* if the line keeps shaking, fracturing? Fracking has caused places in Pennsylvania to be able to light their faucets on fire. Fracking has caused drinking water in Colorado to be so polluted that it is not safe for consumption. Yet we have decided, somewhere along the line, that our water is not important, that our land is not important, that we will continue to worship at the altar of natural gas and crude oil; we will baptize ourselves and live eternally. Are these earthquakes—in this land of political and economic nature—natural? Are we coming closer to the point where politics and economics finally decide that fossil fuels are not worth the earthquakes and pollution that result from their extraction? Will nature ever be separated from politics?

Ohio is not the only place to suffer earthquakes as a result of fracking. Texas has seen them, as well as Arkansas and Oklahoma. England, too. It's one thing to light our water on fire, but the message seems even more clear when the land itself shakes like a beast trying to rid itself of insects on its back. Perhaps the timing of this earthquake is not accidental, as we enter a new year. Perhaps the Good Friday earthquake was not accidental either. Perhaps the Boxing Day earthquake of 2004 that triggered the incredible Indonesian tsunami that killed nearly a quarter million people was a message as well. Are there such things as accidents? What happens if you live your entire life looking for signs? Does God still act in today's world?

In the early 1970s, my grandparents took a trip to Alaska. They both enjoyed history and landscape, and a cruise seemed like the best way to see something new. They brought back scrimshaw and brilliant photographs of Mount McKinley, a signed certificate that made official their crossing the Arctic Circle. But it wasn't all new: my grandfather had spent time at Kodiak Island during the war, when he served in the Coast Guard. He wanted to show my grandmother.

While they were in Anchorage visiting a friend, they heard the story of the Good Friday Earthquake of 1964, when a 9.2 earthquake shook Anchorage like a puppy with a toy. This remains the second-largest earthquake of the twentieth century, surpassed only by the 9.5 earthquake in Chile in 1960. In the twenty-first century, only the 9.1 earthquake in Indonesia in 2004, which killed nearly a quarter-million people, comes close in the modern imagination.

The roads rippled, this friend reports, like waves on the water. The analogy turned to reality when the tsunami hit. The effects of the water were more destructive than the quake in some areas. The water devastated many communities, washed them out to sea. It reshaped Kodiak Island so much that my grandfather did not recognize the place. The USGS website reports that even boats in Louisiana were rocked.

And then, this story, which has become an urban legend: During the quake, those three minutes of intense shaking, fear, exhilaration, adrenaline, and confusion, a mother dashes outside to look for her children. She sees them playing and calls for them to come to her. She tries not to let her fear for them color her voice, but it is there anyway. Her children look up from their play for a moment, debate whether or not to obey. They have lived through earthquakes before. They are common in Alaska, and the children are enjoying the strange internal sensation of wanting to run and wanting to stay put. They cannot decide which is safer. But the panic in their mother's voice penetrates and they leave their toys on the ground and run to her.

The earth opens. A deep fissure, a crack that snakes, and then the snake strikes. The mother watches, screams, horrified as her children fall into the snake's belly. She leaves the safety of her house and runs to them, heedless of the danger, only thinking about saving them. But before she can reach them, the quake stills and the snake retreats to the underworld, taking her children with them. She never sees them again.

When my grandmother tells this story, I shake off its reality. When I search for its authenticity, the USGS website says it can't be true. I don't want it to be true. I don't think of the grief of the mother, the terror of the children; instead, I wonder about the emotional impact of figuratively being swallowed up by the earth. To be so totally wrapped in the environment, like it is a blanket. To understand that what happens to the land also happens to you, that there is nothing to separate you. You breathe the same air, drink the same rain. No longer do you share a symbiotic relationship with the earth. That circle has collapsed into one thin line. Three dimensions no longer exist. What would that intimacy feel like?

Grain Elevator Skyline

August 1984. Five of us are packed into a maroon Pontiac, driving through a blinding rainstorm south to Clara City, Minnesota, for my great-grandmother's funeral. I am five years old; Kristi is three; Kim is eighteen months. Our father is driving; Mom is in the passenger seat. All I remember of my first real introduction to the home of my maternal grandfather is that rainstorm, so heavy that I can't see the hood ornament, and being upstairs in my great-aunt and great-uncle's house, sobbing with the rest of my second cousins, and my mother singing "Children of the Heavenly Father" to calm us down. *Clara City*, the click and the swish of the consonants are the same sounds as the rain and hail on the hood and roof of the car.

In retrospect, the grief I felt was inexplicable because I don't remember my great-grandmother, and we don't have any real connection to the later generations. In 2006, when we again made the pilgrimage to Clara City, this time to bury my grandfather on a cool September day I would rather forget, I felt no real calling to the place the

Kleenes have called home for six generations. When my grandfather went to war in 1943, he left his brother Leonard and the farm, and the land has come down through Leonard's descendants, not ours.

But I want the connection. I want to feel something. I *should* feel something, and because I don't, I feel a bit empty and unworthy. Here is farming country, a land ethic I have no real part of, just a genetic imprint, a kind of birthmark that I cannot see, a birthmark that I neglect to remember for long periods of time, but a marking that links me—and every member of my family—to this piece of land.

This land is both mine and not mine, ambiguous landowning and land-belonging common to every other member of settler cultures in this country, in this space of Minnesota on the border of the Great Plains. I am of the northern Lakes Country, not the farming prairie. My parents are not farmers and neither are my sisters. But I do know what healthy corn is supposed to look like, and I know it's supposed to be knee-high by the Fourth of July. In my Jeep, I know the difference between 4-high and 4-low wheel drive. I know what lutefisk is, what it smells like, and how it moves on a plate—like fish Jell-O—but I have never had the nerve to eat it. I know that lefse, with a little butter and brown sugar, is evidence of the Divine Presence. Where I lived up north, the potatoes thrive in sandy soil, we gleaned in the fields after the harvest was done, and little old Norwegian ladies would take those potatoes to make lefse in the kitchen of the church parish hall. They still tell stories of my father wandering down the hall from his office to sample the rejects, accidentally taking one off the pile of perfect lefse, and all of the ladies screeching at him, *Those aren't the rejects!*—so he poked his finger through it, grinning at them and responding, "Now it is!" I know why deer hunting is essential to the ecology and the economy, and I know why it is important to my father, dressed up every fall in his scratchy wool pants, his red shirt, his rainbow suspenders, his blaze orange jacket, his size-fourteen Gore-Tex boots: not only to spend time with his friends out in the woods he loves so much, but also to fill our freezer with meat for the year when I was growing up.

Down south in Clara City, I know that when I walk through the Lutheran cemetery, I will find names and dates that match my family tree. These are my people, names and histories that have been passed down: Lammert Jansen Ulfert Kleene, who homesteaded this land first, gave the names of the men in his family to his twin boys, Harm and Ulfert. Ulfert, my great-grandfather, named his eldest son Leonard Ulfert after himself, but my grandfather has no family name. Perhaps this made my grandfather's leaving easier.

This place, whether it *was* my place or *is* my place, makes me want to invent a verb tense that incorporates both, the active quality of standing somewhere yet being emotionally elsewhere. I am connected to a place—it's just not *this* place. I breathe easier when I am in the tall Norway pines of north-central Minnesota, where seeing bald eagles is a common occurrence, where loons sing me to sleep at night and wake me in the morning.

And I wonder if there are places on the planet where we connect more strongly to our surroundings, like pulse points. I can feel my heartbeat more strongly if I touch my wrist than if I touch my nose. The geography of the Midwest known as the Heartland grows a mythology of blood and heart, a story we have created for ourselves that tells of a place where the heart beats, the heart of an emerging country, the heart of a people who came to this place looking for home. It is a mythology, this Heartland, one that ignores the realities of how such a land was cleared of its inhabitants and its ecosystems, but it is a mythology that persists.

Here, in Clara City, I feel like I am standing with both feet on the heart of the world.

The existence of the *homeplace* separates the Heartland from other parts of the country, even those places that have formed their own mythology. If the West is adventure and the North is freedom, then the Heartland geography has created a mythology of home. Home can be found anywhere, but the homeplace is different.

The homeplace is where you return, no matter the occasion for gathering. It's where you go for Christmas and Thanksgiving, where your younger sister has always had the job of helping your father put the lights on the Christmas tree, and where middle sister's new husband is given the job of putting the nativity scene together. The first Christmas, he put all the animals in the stable backward and a sheep in the rafters. When he asked your mother what she thought of it, in typical fourth-grade-teacher fashion, she enthusiastically praised his efforts from across the room, not even noticing what he had done. This year, the sheep went in the manger, and the Baby Jesus went into the arms of the Little Drummer Boy.

My homeplace is thirteen miles south of Nevis, in Hubbard County, Minnesota. It is a tiny cabin, seven hundred square feet, designed to be a vacation cabin first, then a retirement home for my grandparents when it became clear that my family would not be moving from Nevis. Most pastors' families move frequently; we were lucky to spend eighteen years in Nevis. The Cabin, in the middle of the Hubbard Prairie, was our place. We did not own our house, the parsonage we lived in, and we could never quite feel at home there. It was not ours. The Cabin is ours. Selling that place would feel like an amputation.

The homeplace is where knowledge and memories live under the same roof, generations of knowledge and memories. Even though my grandfather is gone, my grandmother is in assisted living, and the house is empty, it is still ours. The knotty pine paneling is familiar, and the bedroom where I slept the last time I was there still smells faintly of my grandfather, who has been dead for five years. I know this place intimately, where the poison ivy grows and where the raspberries grow along the roadsides. It is the place where my toddler niece points to the portrait of her great-grandfather and his brother as children and recognizes her own face.

The homeplace is where you go to be buried or to remember where you belong. It's where you can walk the stories of those who share your blood. It's where you can read your own history in the initials carved on the swing tree, in the worn, warm banister, in the nicks on the kitchen floor. It's where you go to remember who you are and where you will find those who will remind you of where you come from. It's where you go to remember what is really important and what is chaff.

Early September is harvest time in northern Minnesota. To the west is sugar beet country. The sugar beet harvest is a twenty-four-hour-a-day process, beginning when the temperature says harvest. If you don't get the beets out of the ground, they rot. The smell of rotting sugar beets is inextricable from this place. The sugar beets like the clay of the Red River Valley; potatoes and beans like the sand of Hubbard County. Soon, we will drive down to Clara City to bury our grandfather in a cemetery surrounded by corn and wheat. We will know what religion a farmer is by the color of his tractor—Clara City has always been divided along religious lines, and there are three dealers of everything in this small town.

The homeplace is where you go to be reminded of what you know.

The homeplace is meant to be inherited. This kind of continuity—avoiding amputation—is essential to the mythology of the Heartland. We all want this grounding of home and the security of home in one way or another. In *Earth Works,* Scott Russell Sanders writes, "Real estate ads offer houses for sale, not homes. A house is a garment easily put off or on, casually bought and sold; a home is a skin. Merely change houses and you will be disoriented; change homes and you bleed."

But a homeplace is not merely a physical place; it is an active mental place as well. Mark Tredinnick writes:

> Home is a verb. Home is the conversation we make with what, and whom, we say we love; a conversation about who we are and always were. Home is a word for the ecology of belonging, and it includes deposition and erosion, the wet and the dry and the cold and the wind; it includes the making and the unmaking, the coming and the going, and it isn't always happy. Sometimes it rains, and sometimes it burns, and sometimes it falls and you fall with it. *(Blue Plateau)*

Perhaps *home* is the verb I want, to span that space between *was* and *is*.

The mythology of the Heartland is one of a simple life, of community. The Heartland is a moral geography, where the land is an expression of the Divine, where "Faith without works is dead" is its motto. It is Laura Ingalls Wilder's *Little House on the Prairie,* not "Little Squatter on the Osage Diminished Reserve," to quote the title of Fran Kaye's article in the *Great Plains Quarterly.* The mythology persists, even in the face of the reality of how the Plains came to be settled. We still love and revere *Little House,* but my adult reading of it is so problematic that I will not give the books to my niece until she is old enough to understand discussions of racism, sexism, and genocide. No questions exist for very long on the prairie; no surprises linger in the land because it has been cultivated, all its natural mystery subtracted to make way for that which is known and controllable. People of the Heartland still reel over the Dust Bowl, feeling that the land betrayed them for reasons they could not understand. The black blizzards and the dusters and the snusters and dust pneumonia became morality tales because that was the only way to understand such wrath and horror.

Control over the land only comes through the most important building block of the land-based mythology of the Heartland: work. Do your part; do not expect that anyone else will do your work. Work builds character; only through character can you really be the person you are meant to be. The way to be truly happy is to be a value to those around you. Anything can be achieved by hard work. What matters is what you do with your own hands—and there is tremendous satisfaction in this. You can see the fields you planted. You can see the barn your ancestors built. You can see the grain elevators, skyline of the Heartland, full of the grain you planted, cultivated, and harvested, ready to feed the world. You have lines of canned fruit and vegetables on the cellar shelf, put up for the winter when it is time to rest.

This mythology is the way we would draw a place if we were handed a canvas and could paint over the tallgrass, the buffalo grass, the grama, and the bluestem and replace them with corn and wheat, just that easy, without the consequences of destroying the grasses. Timothy Egan, author of *The Worst Hard Time,* writes, "In the spring, the carpet flowered amid the green, and as the wind blew, it looked like music on the ground." The mythology sought to retune the music of the grasslands to a different key, from three sharps to one flat, to change the rhythm from the dance of 6/8 to the march of 4/4. To paint the rain in just the right amounts, clouds that let just enough sun through to grow, not to scorch; wind that pollinates, not uproots. Though this mythology is purely of the imagination, we can't seem to separate ourselves from it.

Naturally, a community grows out of the land and the work ethic that the land provokes, or so the mythology hopes. The toughness, the interconnectedness of things, is all the result of the soil, the impossibility of the sod. The Heartland provided, for most, the opportunity for people to own land, maybe for the first time in their family's history. It was Manifest Destiny, the physical embodiment of the American Dream. It meant freedom—which strikes me as ironic, because who is more tied down than a farmer? Who is more conscious of his place in the scheme of things, more aware of how his actions affect other people? Who is willing to sacrifice more, suffer more?

In October 1947, when he was about thirty, my grandfather's brother Leonard lost four fingers on his right hand in a corn picker. My grandfather recalled that they only had a few rows left to go in the field when the picker jammed and Leonard tried to fix it. As my grandfather told the story to me, my grandmother added that her own grandfather and her uncle had both lost fingers to corn pickers or corn huskers. Later, she told me that Leonard had also had an accident that severed his Achilles tendon while he was trying to free some horses from wire and that one of my grandfather's uncles had died young in a farm accident.

What caught me most about these stories is that losing a part of yourself, although not expected, was not surprising to the farmers and their communities. It was a question of *when,* not *if.* What would it be like to be a farmer and know you have a better than even chance to end up on your deathbed without all the parts you were born with? Just this fall, I have heard stories of my high school English teacher, retired now, who had an accident on his farm that broke loose his upper jaw from his skull and broke his lower jaw in four places. A couple of days later, I heard about a high school friend's father who got caught in a swather. What is that mentality like? How can you approach losing fingers, hands, arms with such a cavalier attitude? I suppose the point is much larger—did Leonard quit farming after the accident? Say "I can't do it anymore"? No, he did not. He would have been letting down the people who depended on him, and in the scheme of Heartland mythology, the self is expendable. My grandfather said that Leonard was back in a month, though my grandfather—himself also expendable—commuted for several months from his teaching job to help until Leonard was back to full strength.

There is a commitment found in the Heartland to the land as well as the people who live on it. And this commitment cannot easily be broken—the soil is not just under your fingernails, gritty in your teeth. The soil becomes blood.

When my sisters and I were little, Grandpa would often stop the car, moo to the cows in the field, and they would moo back. But it was my mother who taught me how to tell what kind of cows they were. When I was two or three, she would come up with the Cow Game to keep me occupied. Black and white Holsteins. White-faced Herefords. Brown Jerseys. Black Angus. And it was my Californian father, who has no farming in his blood at all, who came up with the Farm Machinery Game, teaching me what color of tractor was which brand. This was important information, because in Clara City, the town was clearly divided between the Catholic, the Lutheran, and the Dutch Reformed. The town had three grocery stores, three car dealerships, three farm machinery dealers—one for each religion. You could tell which religion people were by the color of the tractor they were driving. We learned why the sandy Hubbard Prairie grew the crops it did—soybeans, corn, strawberries, potatoes—and why those plants liked sandy soil rather than the rich clay of the Red River Valley to the west.

This past Thanksgiving, I carried my twenty-month-old blond sprite of a niece while we picked out a Christmas tree for my parents' house. Cora's gotten very good at animal noises since the last time I saw her, and so when we heard cows mooing from where we were contemplating Fraser fir or white pine, she looked at me and said *Cow.* I nodded. *Want to go see the cow?* Her tiny body stiffened on my hip into one board-straight line. *No.* But she is being raised in Minneapolis, learning what it means to grow up in the city, and even though she is very good at identifying animals, she probably has never seen them in person. Certainly she had never seen a cow and didn't know what a Red Angus looked like or the sounds they made.

She did relax when she could put a cow face with the sound it made, making tiny mooing sounds in my ear as she cuddled close, still unsure about these red, long-faced animals. *Moo,* she said. *Moo.* When we returned to my parents' house, my youngest sister put her hands to her mouth like Grandpa used to, making a mooing sound while flapping one hand for the correct vibrato. *Moooo.* It was an excellent imitation of Grandpa, and we all missed him fiercely at that moment, even as we laughed.

My maternal great-grandmother cooked from dawn till dusk for the threshers, and was famous for it, but neither of her daughters became farmer's wives. My great-aunt was the first in the family not only to graduate from high school but also to attend and graduate from college. My grandmother followed suit, so did my mother, so did my sisters and I. In the same way, on my father's side of the family, a family where life has not been dependent on the land for many generations, the women—my grandmother, my great-grandmother, my great-great-grandmother—were all able to choose a career outside the home, to travel, even to choose not to be married, things that the women of my mother's family would never have dreamed of.

Even though we had been separated from our farming roots, we didn't escape them completely. I remember my mother keeping a garden for much of my childhood, and my sisters planted a garden every spring. Tomatoes, green beans, carrots, potatoes, beets, squash. I remember our dog, a beautiful beagle-springer mix named Katy, delicately snipping green beans off the plants and taking them to the shade of the plum tree to eat. I remember her snatching a carrot off the pile my mother had just unearthed, propping it between her paws like a venison bone my father had stored for her in the freezer from the previous fall.

Once the vegetables were harvested, my mother and grandparents would set up shop in the kitchen. Grandpa would cut up the beans, beets, or carrots. They were blanched and then dried between layers of bath towels. The veggies went into plastic bags and into the freezer for the winter. The beans and carrots always got eaten first, leaving the beets and squash that we hated for February and March. The only saving grace of the beets was trying to eat as many as it would take to change the color of our pee.

My grandmother cannot understand this recent obsession her granddaughters have with canning. Why would you want to can when you don't have to? It's long, sweaty work. But my youngest sister, just twenty-four, bought tomatoes at a farmer's market, took them home to Mom, and they canned nearly twenty quart jars of tomatoes. Then Kim bought a half-bushel of the quintessential Minnesota apple, Haralson. Mom went to visit her in Minneapolis, and they made applesauce and canned it. Preserving food has become as much a political statement about wanting to know what goes into our food as it is an economic decision. Even though times have changed enough so that barn raisings and quilting bees are not part of our social structure in the Heartland, we still have our ways: potluck dinners after church, community fund-raisers for those in trouble. Food is how we counter the fear of change in the Heartland.

We fear the change of a baby from fetus to premature infant; we fear the change of life into death, especially when the change is not natural or expected. We fear the change of living comfortably to possessing only the burned-out shell of a house. We fear that our lives will change economically or physically, and we will become less fortunate. We mask this fear by sharing food, affirming that we are still alive. We bring food after tragedy, after death, to sustain the life that still remains. Even now, in many small-town churches in the Heartland, you will find yourself sitting down to lunch in the fellowship hall after a funeral, something I haven't experienced in the larger places I have lived. In *Grass Roots,* Paul Gruchow, the Minnesota essayist, writes:

> The prairie is a community. It is not just a land-
> scape or the name of an area on a map, but a
> dynamic alliance of living plants, animals, birds,
> insects, reptiles, and microorganisms, all depend-
> ing on each other. When too few of them remain,
> their community loses its vitality and they perish
> together. The prairie teaches us that our strength
> is in our neighbors. The way to destroy a prairie
> is to cut it up into tiny pieces, spaced so that they
> have no communication.

When I visited my grandparents a few summers ago, they took me to the American Legion for dinner, where there was a benefit for the hospice. Seven dollars for chicken, mashed potatoes, gravy, beans, cranberry sauce, and lemonade. And for dessert, vanilla ice cream and your choice of strawberry, chocolate, or caramel syrup. As we feasted, my grandparents filled me in on the doings of various people we saw. From a distance, there is something very comforting about everybody knowing everybody's business. It can be harmful, but it also helps keep feet out of mouths. There is a reason we are connected, why we should be, why we have to be. Quite simply, it keeps us alive. The Heartland takes that mandate very seriously, but it takes most things very seriously.

It was probably dark by the time we pulled into Clara City for my great-grandmother's funeral. I don't remember. I don't have the memories anymore. I don't know where we spent the night, or even if we came down the night before. Leonard and Lily Mae were no longer living on the farm by that time, so we all congregated at their house in town. The farm was their son Gerald's. I want to imagine what happened.

We pull into the driveway. All the lights are on. Lily Mae has been looking out for us. So has Gram—worrying about us driving through that terrible storm. But the storm has moved on now, and they can see the heavy black front move east, leaving that unearthly light of the sunset in its wake. The light always seems so strange after that darkness, and my parents stand there for a moment and look. Lily Mae and Gram come out of the front door, ready to help take care of sweet, sleepy children. Lily Mae takes Kim, Gram takes Kristi, and Dad takes me. Mom follows, threading through the throngs of her relatives gathered in little groups around the house. It is good that everybody is here, even under the circumstances. They settle the kids upstairs with some of the rest of the little ones. Some of the other women are up there. Then the adults go downstairs to connect and reconnect.

Dishes of food cover every flat space. Everyone brings food when someone dies. All the cousins are there, all the extended relatives, good friends. They tell stories of Bianca. They tell stories of her sons and her grandchildren. There is laughter and tears, all of which solidifies the family and the community. Tomorrow, Bianca will be laid to rest. The Heartland will welcome her home, and she will become part of the heartbeat.

I-90

Heading Home to Third Crow Wing Lake:
Thirteen Hours from Home

The black of the sky is as dense as the black under my tires, broken only by the occasional lightning white of oncoming headlights. We are past the threshold of time where late becomes early, but the sky has not yet begun to lighten, and I feel a strange comfort in this cocoon of untime. This is the point of time before the world is fully awake. Those who are awake are thoroughly caffeinated. In the passenger seat, I have two Stanley thermoses filled with cheap Earl Grey spiked with lemon. My travel mug with its Cabela's Outfitters cozy is in my cup holder, the tea too hot to drink.

It is 5:00 a.m., and I just crossed the Ohio–Indiana border, heading west on I-80/90. From my home in Bowling Green, Ohio, where I have been living since I moved from Spokane, it takes about an hour on the Ohio Turnpike to reach the border. For me, 4:00 a.m. is that threshold where late becomes early. The toll costs $2.35. Somewhere in Indiana, I will fill up the gas tank, even though it's not empty, and I will use the bathroom, even though I'm not full. Experience has taught me that trying to get through Chicago without this stop is not a good idea. Twelve hours after the Lake Forest Oasis on the west end of Chicago, I will arrive at my parents' doorstep in northern Minnesota, the land of my childhood. It seems important to make this distinction, that my adulthood is on one end of my driving day and my childhood is on the other. It's an ugly drive, sixteen hours, but it is doable, and I have done it so many times that all the trips seem to run together into one single thread of road.

My perception of I-90 doesn't start at zero in Seattle and end at 3111.52 in Boston; because of this, sometimes I-90 is more metaphorical than literal. It means I-80/90 from Bowling Green, Ohio, to Chicago, where I-80 splits off and heads for Iowa and Nebraska, which I will call home in a few years. I-90 picks up I-94 and they coexist peacefully until Wisconsin, when I-90 moves south and eventually scores the land of southern Minnesota. I stay on I-94 and it takes me through the Twin Cities; north of the Cities, I leave I-94 at St. Cloud and follow Highway 10 north to Nevis (via Hwy 64) or Detroit Lakes (where my parents currently live). If I'm continuing west, I'll stay on Highway 10 until it intersects with I-94 again, which will take me to Fargo–Moorhead, where I went to college, forty-five miles west of Detroit Lakes. I'll cruise on I-94 through North Dakota and Montana until it meets up with I-90, then I'll follow I-90 through Montana, Idaho, and Washington. My I-90 ends twenty miles west of Spokane.

There's an importance to the road, to any road. There's a relationship formed between road and driver, one that sometimes seems to defy consciousness. Some drive because getting from point A to point B means food for their family. Some drive because it is the lesser of several traveling evils. And some drive because they have to, because there is something elemental in that meeting of tire and asphalt that isn't satisfied any other way. But motor vehicle travel exhausts me and makes me cranky, so I don't like to do it—especially if it is an extended amount of time. However, if I-90 is involved, that's a different story. And it is a story, quite literally—one that boasts its own sound track.

In my narrow world, I-90 matters because this is the fastest way to get where I want to go, home. There's music attached to I-90, music that cannot be separated from the road, and this is special. It's like listening to a movie's sound track and knowing exactly what is happening on the screen just by the music. The same is true of I-90. The sound track to I-90 is like paint lines on the asphalt—natural, expected, guiding, and if they weren't there, you would drive off the road because your sense of direction would be skewed. By listening to the sound track of the road, you know where you are. This is what happens when you follow a road that is literal as well as figurative and are conscious enough to listen to the song.

Deep in the Australian Aboriginal creation myths, in the time "just before the land was entirely awake," long before I-90 was a gleam in Eisenhower's eye, the Ancestors came up from the earth and walked across the land. David Abrams details this "Dreamtime" in his book *The Spell of the Sensuous,* and he writes that the Ancestors didn't just walk, "they sang their way across the land." This idea is so wonderful that I loved this story long before

I knew I-90. *The Ancestors sang their way across the land. They sang to a world that was in that beautiful, lulled space between sleep and waking.* I knew what that felt like, sounded like, meant. Tens of thousands of years after the Dreamtime, when my sisters and I were little, my grandfather, a full-blooded German Minnesotan, was often given the task of walking us to sleep. We were not sit-in-a-rocker babies, I am told. I have early memories of him pacing the living room floor with my youngest sister, singing "Go Tell Aunt Rhody." When he ran out of verses, and Kim was still at full steam, he would start over. Walking and singing, walking and singing, imprinting his voice, his music, onto our deepest subconscious. He had a lovely baritone voice, so I imagine that we liked the feel of his voice vibrating in his chest as he held us to him, walking and singing, walking and singing. This, I suppose, was the Dreamtime in reverse, waking to sleeping, instead of the other way around.

The Ancestral Dreaming tracks are not simply a road. They are more than a musical road map that shows the Aborigines how to get from point A to point B; more important, each step is a naming of things, tangible reminiscences of what stories lay along the road from previous trips. The Dreaming tracks are as much a literal path to tangible places as they are the history of a people, histories written in song. A fresh spring might be a chorus. A hill might be a couplet, rhyming and rhythmic. Each Ancestor's step a note, each stumble a minor chord.

This is how my I-90 that isn't always I-90 became a Songline. There are other minor Songlines on the highways and dirt roads around where I grew up in Hubbard County in northern Minnesota, but they aren't as important as this one. I-90 is the point from which everything else comes—and if you don't know where you come from, you can't know where the path will go. But the importance of northern Minnesota is more than the midpoint on the Songline. It is the artery through which my blood flows. I went west after college, to Spokane. After Spokane, I went east and landed in Ohio. But never too far from the Songline. No matter which direction I choose to point my car, it will always lead me home.

Before the Land Was Entirely Awake:
Driving West, September 2001

To be perfectly honest, I hate driving I-94 from Minnesota through North Dakota and Montana as much as I hate I-80/90 through Indiana. I don't know how many times I have driven this stretch of the west, from Minnesota to Spokane, but it is a very long, very boring drive. It is two days of twelve-hour drives, and that is rough on anybody. The first time I drove the I-90 that was still I-94, I had just graduated from college. I was moving out to Spokane for more education. A few days after my father and I arrived in Spokane and my college friend Matt (the only soul I knew in Spokane) helped us move into my first apartment, the world would be shaken by 9/11, and I would be standing in my first home with no outside communication. If home is a place to feel safe, what was I doing in Spokane by myself? That night, Matt, probably feeling as scared as I was, brought pizza over and things were okay, at least for that stretch of time.

Following a Songline, even if it is a freeway, promotes this connectedness to what we hold dear—and the medium is the music. It is just as effective as holding a map made of paper. And you don't have to worry about folding a song back into the glove compartment. Walking and singing, driving and singing. The road, the sound track, the map of the world, becomes even more clear when it is a family member who is doing the singing. Such music connects the people involved as closely as it connects human to road—and being connected, not existing alone, is the point.

The first time I drove the Songline to Spokane, in 2001, Dad was towing a trailer containing everything I owned with the Suburban and I was following in my 1998 Oldsmobile Achieva. The year after I moved from Spokane, my sister and I drove from Nevis to Missoula—sixteen hours—in one day because she had a job interview there, and the following three hours to Spokane the next day. And the last time on this Songline, in 2005, the entire family populated our parents' Suburban. Three adult girls, two parents. We hadn't had a family trip together since I graduated from high school. My youngest sister had just graduated from college, so we were going to be even more geographically scattered than we had been. We were imprinting every memory on our bones and singing loud enough to echo off the prairies, off the mountains.

Certainly the finer point of the whole concept of the Songlines is to keep a person connected to the earth as much as it is to keep a person connected to those around him or her. Given the traditional Genesis creation story, humans were created from the earth, the clay. The land is not as inert and as dead as we sometimes believe—or more accurately, we don't often consider that the soil could be alive. We come from the earth, and we return to the earth. That should be enough to explain why we can feel at home in places we have never been, why we can hear a strain of music and instantly be elsewhere, on a specific linear mile of road.

This placement happens when the music fits not only the location, but also the timing and your state of mind. Driving west on I-94 through North Dakota, the Songline tracks my move from Nevis to Spokane, where, in my overly dramatic, twenty-two-year-old, newly graduated-from-college way, I was feeling a need to make a break from my hometown, to consciously move away. I didn't want to end up in my hometown by default, just because I never left. Caedmon's Call, a Christian band that was especially popular at my Lutheran college in the late 1990s, recorded "Faith My Eyes," which expressed how I expected to relate to my hometown, which would never again be my home: *Hometown weather's on TV / I imagine the lives of the people living there / And I'm curious if they imagine me.* No other place could be home. But the only way to really know that was to deliberately leave and then to return—and I was feeling a bit self-righteous about leaving. The acoustic guitar lead is too complicated for a guitarist of my limited skill, but it is gentle and sentimental. The male vocal isn't a powerhouse of a voice, which enhances the simplicity of the overall tune. *So keep 'em coming, these lines on the road.* Keep 'em coming, one foot in front of the other, toward making a home of my own. Driving east toward Minnesota, I don't hear Caedmon's Call, because I am not leaving home—I am heading toward it.

On that early September afternoon in 2001, by the time Dad and I cross the border from North Dakota into Montana at Beach—a place-name that always makes me laugh—I have driven through the sentimentality of what I have left behind, and I am dead center in my second thoughts. But I can't turn around now. I would look like an idiot. The sound track of the Songline becomes more complex. You know you've found the Songline when the music suits the location as well as the timing and your state of mind. "Wide Open Spaces" by the Dixie Chicks is my North Dakota–Montana anthem for leaving home and being strong enough to face new people, new challenges, new mistakes, new successes. *It takes the shape of a place out west / But what it holds for her, she hasn't yet guessed.* I've passed the halfway point of the drive, and I am going to be settling in Washington State, past which there isn't any more West. And perhaps there is a chord of cliché here, for this song to be attached to this part of the road, but I don't care. It's my Songline. And for one who has never felt particularly brave, this stretch of the Songline is a spine-strengthening *hoo-yah!* The lead female vocal is in my vocal range, so I belt out the lyrics at the top of my lungs. *She needs wide open spaces.* She needs to move away so that she has somewhere to return to. She needs to know that the road that takes her away will also lead her back. Instead of feeling clichéd, I feel connected.

Even after I moved away from Spokane, I could still hear these strains on this part of the Songline as I drove west, and it made me smile.

Once I-94 meets up with I-90 and I-94 ends, the road picks up Storyhill's "I-90." The acoustic duo pound their guitars and rough harmonies through the speakers. I almost expect the speaker coverings to fray and catch fire. I even think I smell a bit of smoke. It's a live recording, so screams from the audience match the drive of the lyrics and the fierceness of the delivery. Of course, part of my love for this song is the mention of a Minnesota gal, which I am. Few sing about Minnesota girls, so the novelty drags me along.

Soon I'll be hightailin' I-90 . . .

And so the Songline goes, my map for finding my way in the world.

Fourth of July Pass, Idaho:
Driving East, June 2002

I might prefer to walk my Songlines, to be wrapped in the deeply buried memories of my grandfather carrying me along his Songline, but once I moved to Spokane after college, the Songlines were no longer walkable. The separation, not surprisingly, hurt. My Songlines were only driveable, only discernible under the tires of my car. I had two twelve-hour days of driving before I could be home in Minnesota, and I was eager to feel the road under my tires.

Bruce Chatwin, in his work *The Songlines,* observes, "To some, the Songlines were like the Art of Memory in reverse," as each note of the Songline was a specific, physical place. I didn't consciously understand how the Songlines could be written in the road until I drove I-90 through the 4th of July Pass in Idaho, on my way home. Learning the westward melodies would come on the return to Spokane.

On this morning, at sunrise, the 4th of July Pass was the first cymbal crash of the Songline onto my consciousness. This art of memory was leading me home, to the place where the key signature of my blood matched the staff and notes of the roads in Hubbard County and the small towns of my childhood—Park Rapids, Laporte, Nevis—and every path between them.

The elements of sunrise, driving east, and summer harmonize and echo off the mountains. The rough texture of Mac Powell's voice in Third Day's powerful southern-rock rendition of "Agnus Dei" abrades my skin, a band that sounds suspiciously like Hootie and the Blowfish. I decide that the distortion of the electric guitar is just enough to get my nerve endings up so that I am sensitive to every nuance of everything around me. *Hallelujah . . . Hallelujah . . .* The harmonies heat my blood; the guitar riffs are heavy with awe. The sun was coming up over the mountains as I drove through—it was nothing like any other sunrise I had ever driven through. There wasn't anything particularly unique about it, but it was one of the most glorious. "Agnus Dei" was the perfect sound track for the moment. Memories of Third Day were left over from my college experience as well as my work at a Lutheran Bible camp during the summers. The bass line, moving from Cs to Fs, the crisp snare of the drum, then the blast of the electric lead. Good God, I thought, my mind swept clean of everything but the music and the sunrise. Then the density of the accompaniment drops off to the drums, light lead, and a single, rough, male vocal line. The guitars, the bass, these form the harmonies with the solo melody line. The effect was as staggering as the mountains I was driving through.

In the middle of the song, the vocal line and the instruments fade out, leaving only Mac's voice to carry the single note, a moment of silence that could signal the end of the song but doesn't—and then the music explodes back, with a crash of guitars and drums, accompanied by other voices, layered in harmony. The sunlight seems to intensify at this point, and my blood heats even further. The mountain pass, the angle of sunlight, the music—it is all stamped permanently on this stretch of road. There is no other road to which this song clings. This is, quite simply, the music of the sunrise. It is all right here. Only here.

Singing the world into being. I would have liked to have been present at such a creation.

I had to test the theory, to make sure that my fanciful nature wasn't overtaking my good sense; I wanted to play the song on the same place in the road, but while driving in a different direction at a different time of day and then see what would happen. In 2005 I drove with my parents and adult sisters west through the 4th of July Pass in the afternoon, driving toward Holden Village in Washington State. As we passed the sign that indicated our position, I started the track on the CD. My sister Kristi, who once crossed the pass with me at sunrise under the auspices of "Agnus Dei," said what was I thinking: Disappointing. We needed east and sunrise, not west in the afternoon. I once drove east at sunrise out of Iowa City and cranked up the volume on "Agnus Dei," just in case I was mistaken about the geography of the song. I sighed heavily as the miles and notes went by. The song only works at sunrise when you are driving east through the 4th of July Pass, with the windows rolled down to let the chill of the dawn wind skim across your skin, blasting the music and letting it echo off the mountains.

Out of Bowling Green: Driving West on I-80/90

Driving west feels like going downhill, especially when Minnesota is my destination. West is easy and natural—and I am not driving into the blinding sunrise on the prairie. The magnet of *home* is very strong, for the familiarity not only of people but of roads. I want to drive the back roads and know exactly where I am going and how I am going to get there. This is the true test of home: if you know it intimately, you will know how to get from point A to point B by at least four or five different paths. In Hubbard County, I know the roads. I know all the ways to get home after the Fourth of July fireworks in Park Rapids, avoiding all the main roads, avoiding all the secondary roads that even some of the tourists know about, and heading straight for the tertiary roads.

Though it lasts only for the first few miles out of my Bowling Green driveway, the first song along the eastern end of the Songline is Shooter Jennings's "Gone to Carolina"—but my sisters and I modified it to "Gone to Minnesota." (Faith Hill's "Mississippi Girl," likewise, has become "Minnesota Girl.") I-90 will lead me home, after all. The earthy nature of the southern rock, the mix of rough voice, the smoky guitar licks, all make me wish that I was from the South, that this music was part of my blood from the beginning. Crank up the volume. I don't want to dance; I want to absorb. I want to live inside that guitar. I want this music to seep into my pores, color my skin, change my open Minnesota vowels to soft southern consonants.

Not too bad a motivator at 4:00 a.m.

I pull out of Bowling Green and barely pass the last stoplight when an unearthly sound emanates from the passenger seat. I have been expecting this. From experience, I know that the cat will keep this up for two hours, and then he will be fine. I will coo and soothe until we hit I-80/90, the Ohio Turnpike, and then I will give up and chug my caffeine and turn up the volume on *anything* to keep me awake. But I can't sing with all the music I have chosen, even if they are my favorite songs. I don't know why.

The sound track of this stretch of I-90 is mostly the grinding of my teeth. Even when I time this to miss most of Chicago's morning rush hour, it is still too much traffic for me. When I am not grinding my teeth, I am muttering. The trick to traffic is to stay calm and crank up the volume on Eric Clapton's version of "Sweet Home Chicago." Failing that, exercise the adult vocabulary. I don't usually swear too much in daily life, but set me down in heavy traffic, and you will mistake me for a sailor. There is no freedom to this road. Not in literal or figurative terms, given the toll stops. Music does not stick to this stretch of the road.

There is an exception, eight minutes' worth. Somewhere between Chicago and Milwaukee, Third Day blasts the complex guitar layers of "Give." Something about this band matches this road. The beat, the bass line, the roughness of Mac Powell's voice, it all gets into my blood, which makes my body groove in the driver's seat, sets an imaginary guitar pick into my right hand to strum along with the band. There is something elemental about the fourth interval, from C to F, D to G, and so on. I can't quite explain it. But something about that particular interval goes beyond hearing into physically feeling the music dead center in your chest. It lodges there, and it resonates. Vibrates a little. When I hit Milwaukee, it is gone. I can play the song again and again, but it doesn't have the same groove. And neither do I.

To cure myself of the boredom that this portion of the Songline offers so effortlessly, I switch to audiobooks. Being mentally involved in the story I am listening to keeps me from dwelling on the fact that no matter how I might wish it otherwise, Wisconsin will always be five hours long. I don't know why it took me so long to catch on that the Ancestors must not have passed this way. I don't listen to much music when I am on long stretches of road anymore.

Through Hudson, Wisconsin, West on I-94:
Back in Minnesota

I am four hours away from home, and I am both exhausted and antsy.

Once I-90 splits off and I am following I-94, things always brighten a bit—even if it is dark or raining. I can't listen to a book when I am in traffic, so after I pass Hudson, Wisconsin, and cross over the gorgeous St. Croix River into familiar Minnesota country, I push Jars of Clay's *The Eleventh Hour* album into the player, another remnant of my high school and college years, which I haven't listened to much since. The songs of this album are attached to this stretch of the Songline because it is usually literally the eleventh hour of my driving, with one more to go before I arrive at my sisters' doorstep.

I am almost there.

I-90 isn't as linear as I would like to make it. Certainly it is a two-dimensional sound track, a Dreaming track that shows me how to go where I need to go. I followed it west, over landscapes that I never considered calling my own. Whether or not Spokane suited me, whether or not I could call that patch of eastern Washington home, doesn't really matter. It is a chorus on my sound track, a freshwater spring, a cache of food. From there, it was natural to drive east to find myself at the beginning of the song, up north in Hubbard County, where the roads sang a different tune. Perhaps I overcompensated and ended up east of Minnesota, on I-90 in Ohio. Perhaps I am just stretching, to see how far I can get away from home and still know who I am. The west was not as difficult as the east, I have found. The east is very hard. The need to go west, to go home, to find myself on the roads I know, is more compelling.

At the Intersection of U.S. Highway 10 and Minnesota Highway 64: Heading North, an Hour from Home

My ancestors singing their way across the land really meant singing their way across the living room floor, so my first solid introductions to music, with my head against my grandfather's chest, was at blood level. I lean toward the literal when I believe that music is in the blood. There is rhythm in everything. Me, I cook to Aretha Franklin, clean to the Three Tenors, rage to Carl Orff's *Carmina Burana,* concentrate to anything jazz. But the most soothing music is that with a beat that matches the beat of a heart at rest. About sixty beats per minute. That can't be coincidence.

Applying this idea to the road and the reality of the Songlines isn't that far off, since both earth and blood represent life. The road is an extension of the earth, more obvious sans asphalt. In *Songlines,* Chatwin observes, "When [the Aborigines] wished to thank the earth for its gifts, they would simply slit a vein in their forearms and let their own blood spatter the ground." The Aboriginal idea of conception involves both the earth and music, combining these ideas within the framework of a family. The Aborigines believed that as the Ancestors were singing their way across the land, they deposited "spirit children" in their wake. Intercourse only prepared a woman for a child and the actual conception was the result of her stepping on an Ancestor's song couplet. Music is blood, literally, within the context of the Aboriginal ideas.

I am in love with that idea—the blood in the baby's veins being music. It follows that the land is music, music that results in conceiving a child—and children are born into families. A memory bank for finding one's way around. A map for the road ahead. Such would be part of a family's function in the universe. When my sister was pregnant with my niece, a family friend gave them her piano, which promptly went into their dining room, the center of their house. My sisters separated their piano books from Mom's, brought them to Minneapolis, and my present to Kristi during month two was a book of piano music that contained our favorite arrangement of "Ode to Joy." Cora probably heard this song before she heard any others, back when she was the size of a kidney bean. These days, the first notes of that arrangement will send her delightedly spinning in circles, her eighteen-month-old idea of dancing. She also likes to crawl onto the piano bench, flip through the *Reader's Digest* book of childrens' songs, and request "The Cow Song," which is really "Bingo."

As lifelong Lutherans, we probably sang before we could talk. Garrison Keillor wrote a humorous little piece called "Singing with the Lutherans" that slips its truth in so easily that I feel like I have always known this:

> Lutherans are bred from childhood to sing in
> four-part harmony. It's a talent that comes from
> sitting on the lap of someone singing alto or tenor
> or bass and hearing the harmonic intervals by
> putting your little head against that person's rib
> cage. It's natural for Lutherans to sing in harmony.
> We're too modest to be soloists, too worldly to
> sing in unison. When you're singing in the key of
> C and you slide into the A7th and D7th chords, all
> two hundred of you, it's an emotionally fulfilling
> moment.

There is something about singing in harmony that promotes a sense of unity, and within a family—blood-related or religious—that unity and connectedness is the most important way we support each other. Ladysmith Black Mambazo's rendition of "Precious Lord, Take My Hand," my grandfather's favorite hymn, the one we sang at his funeral, which can still bring me to tears over that memory, is one of the most incredible moments of music recorded—the harmony, the distance between the first and fourth chords, the threads of African rhythm, the bass line that resonates in my own chest. Keillor mentions learning harmonic intervals by putting your head against someone's rib cage. I wonder if Cora is learning harmony as she lays her head against my chest.

I have had more moments like this than I can count, particularly the first time I heard the Doxology sung at half the speed I am used to singing it. Each note is eight beats, one whole breath. *Praise God from whom all blessings flow.* After the first few notes in unison, the group spontaneously splits into harmony, some finding the higher notes, some going low. My eyes widened in surprise, but it felt like my entire body was expanding. I felt like a balloon, my skin elastic, my body becoming lighter, my skin tingling with something I couldn't understand. Keillor's "emotionally fulfilling" hardly seems enough. Every time since has generated a similar reaction. Goosebumps prickle, my scalp tingles, and I am filled with an awe so great that I am speechless for several moments past the end of the song. I am not the only one so affected. Location, timing, state of mind—this is what makes music stick.

How could such simplicity be transformed into something so incredible? Because the music has transcended the auditory and connected itself on a cellular level to our blood? What happens when you stand on a song couplet and make it auditory? What happens when you drive over a song couplet and let your tires follow the chorus for a while? How many possible connections can be made that go beyond song and road, between song and road and human, between song and human and human? And where will you be if you let those connections fuel your car? What will that home-place look like? Will that matter, if you know that the road will lead you back?

And so I fire up my truck, pull back onto the road, and see where Storyhill's song will take me.

Soon I'll be hightailin' I-90.

Ballerina in a Snowsuit

I

Phyllis Olson was seventeen years old, a willowy girl with curly brown hair and water-blue eyes, tough in ways only a girl who lived through the Depression, descended from four generations of Swedes in the farming country of eastern Minnesota, could be. She spoke English as her first language, the first generation of her family to do so. Her parents spoke English, but they spoke Swedish around each other, especially when they did not want their children to know what they were talking about. On November 11, 1940, Armistice Day, she was attending her first year of college at St. Cloud State Teacher's College.

Her father, Harry, the oldest of nine children, called her Lolly, and he was one of many young men from Chisago County who had been drafted to fight in the Great War. He never saw combat and came home to learn that his four-day honeymoon with his bride had resulted in his first daughter, named Harriet after him. He, probably more than anyone else in his family, appreciated what Armistice Day meant. He had an uncle who fought in the Spanish-American War twenty years before the Great War, and a grandfather who fought in the Civil War—so Harry probably had heard stories about what would have been in store for him in those trenches in France, had he gotten there. But what did he know of war anyway, beyond stories? He was a farmer, descended from farmers, and that is all he would ever be. Maybe Harry liked the idea of war as his only chance for adventure outside the farm. He knew what awaited him when he returned.

November 1940. War is on everyone's mind. The United States is still officially neutral to the skirmishes of Europe. Phyllis's generation, born in the years after the Great War, talks of grand absolutes. Harry's generation knows what the Germans are capable of, that maybe the Armistice wasn't the solution they all hoped it would be. Rations? They had lived through the Depression and the Dust Bowl, those times when Harry would drink away the milk money on the way home from the creamery. Rations were not a frightening prospect. They lived close enough to the bone as it was, as if they were already on rations.

   November 1940. Tacoma, Washington. A storm blows up over the Pacific, nothing terribly spectacular for this time of year. The new suspension bridge over the Tacoma Narrows to Gig Harbor has been open since July, a marvel of modern engineering, the third-largest suspension bridge in the world. But folks noticed that the slightest whiff of a breeze would set the bridge to shaking. The gale-force winds of November 7 caught the bridge at the right frequency and turned it into a ribbon of taffy, with cars and people still on it. Resonance, engineers say, harmonic intervals. Later, when I learned about the Australian Songlines, about roads written in music, I would think of the Tacoma Narrows Bridge.

The winds played crack the whip with this marvel of modern engineering, then snapped it, cable by cable, twisted it like a rope, and tossed it into the water. The marvel was not simply that the bridge—nicknamed Galloping Gertie—collapsed; it was that no humans died, though a dog in a car perished, and that it was caught on film.

The question may be, *How can you fight what you cannot see?*

Later, meteorologists would use terms like cyclonic and panhandle hook—a type of storm that would sink the *Edmund Fitzgerald* in 1975. During this storm, several ships on the Great Lakes sank, and mariners talked about the Witch of November. Minnesotans talked about duck hunters, caught by surprise by the unexpected arrival of the storm. After the Armistice Day Blizzard, the National Weather Service—whose regional headquarters were in Chicago—changed the way it forecasted its predictions.

II

In the cemetery in Seward, Nebraska, just twenty minutes from Lincoln, a gray obelisk marks the final resting place of Etta Shattuck, who was nineteen when she died in 1888, after saving several of her pupils from freezing to death in the storm that is called the Children's Blizzard. David Laskin's heartbreaking book *The Children's Blizzard* considers not only the human toll of this blizzard—at least 235 people, most of them children—but also the advances that the National Weather Service implemented in the aftermath. We did learn something from this blizzard, after all. U.S. Poet Laureate Ted Kooser put the voices of those lost into poetry in *Blizzard Voices*. Ron Hansen's short story "Wickedness" tilts my world on its axis every time I read it. There are more ways to tell this story than there are snowflakes.

The story goes like this: It had been a very hard winter, with temperatures so brutal that most of the school-age children had been kept home for several weeks. On this bright January day, the cold snap broke; the temperature rose to a few degrees above freezing, not only delighting the children—and their mothers who shooed them off to school—but the adults who could safely venture out to take care of their farms. But over the course of the day, January 12, a moisture-heavy front from the Gulf smashed into a cold front from the north, and the temperatures dropped nearly fifty degrees within a few hours. The snow raged, the wind whipped, and all tried to find shelter where they could. Most of the children had gone to school without their coats because it had been so warm that morning, and teachers frantically tried to keep them warm, to keep them alive. Some children who set off for home before the storm hit never made it; some were badly frostbitten. Etta Shattuck, one of the teachers, took refuge in a haystack and survived, but the frostbite was bad enough that her legs needed to be amputated, and she died a few days later. This blizzard is littered with tales of survival, of heroism, of near misses, of missed opportunities, of life and death and everything that a human being is capable of.

The ground in front of her gravestone was frozen the day I stood in front of it, the sky a clear, cold blue—and I had no idea what to think, how to recognize, even to myself, the collision of such forces and what happens when such things we cannot see and cannot comprehend come up against the force of the human spirit.

Snow and wind and winter are part of my world because I choose to live in places where winter means snow. But it will always remain a mystery to me, and to some degree, a site of laughter and joy, even as it reminds me of blizzards that have names, ice that has sent my Jeep and me into a ditch, storms that have killed friends of the family. I still remember the snows of 1997, when Fargo received more than 100 inches of snow, which complicated the spring melt of the Red River, leading to that flood whose scars have not yet faded. Yet the first snowfall of the year always makes me smile.

III

My birthday is near the end of October, and I never remember a childhood birthday that did not have snow. I haven't seen snow this early in several years, which disappoints me more than I expected it to, especially as Halloween approaches. Five hundred miles northeast of Lincoln, Nebraska, my twenty-month-old niece Cora is getting ready for her Halloween adventure. She will be a bunny, a fuzzy, pink, full-suited affair that covers her from the top of her head to the tip of her toes. The costume has a belly on it, and, via Skype, Cora proudly shows me that she has learned to hop. Because bunnies *hop,* she tells me, popping the *p.* I want to teach her what a bunny says, because my parents tell the story of someone asking me that question when I was about Cora's age, and my answer was just a wiggle of my nose.

The costume itself is important. It is an appropriate costume for a Minneapolis Halloween, because her parents can layer clothes under it to keep her warm. They are going to only three houses, with her parents, two of her three aunts, and two grandmothers trailing her little bunny tail like paparazzi; going trick-or-treating in Minnesota is never an easy proposition. Two years later, she will be a "magic giraffe," a costume that involved a giraffe costume too small for her—the legs were knee-length—and a wand. I love that kid.

My earliest Halloween memories are in Laporte, Minnesota, the one Halloween where I got to wear my genuine ballet tutu for a costume. Naturally, it wasn't the best idea to walk down the street in tights, leotard, and tutu without a snowsuit because I probably would have frozen before I got to the end of the driveway, but Mom drove us to the school's carnival. Mom usually made most of our costumes, from the marshmallow Kristi was one year (stuffed with newspaper, with a little white hat) to the next year when she dyed it orange, messed with the cap, and it became a pumpkin for Kim. I remember a poodle costume and ubiquitous princess costumes.

My mother, elementary teacher extraordinaire, would always bring home that big paper that comes on a roll, cover the storm door with it, and draw something on it, five somethings. A Daddy ghost, a Mommy ghost, a Karen ghost, a Kristi ghost, and a Kim ghost. Each year it was something different—her creativity knew no bounds. Each one would be our exact height, and when Mom cut out the eyeholes, when the doorbell rang, we could see through to see who was at the door. I thought I had a picture of one of them, but I don't know where it went. My sister Kristi has picked up the tradition at her own house, with her own children.

Since dark comes so early at that time of year, we would eat dinner at 4:30—a treat to eat so early. We carved the pumpkins a day or two before, and they were ready to be lit. We gazed longingly up at the big yellow Tupperware bowl on top of the fridge, already filled with bags of candy, at a height that only Dad could reach. We would make the rounds of our three-hundred-person town and the carnival held at the school. Mom always took us trick-or-treating, and Dad always volunteered to stay home and hand out candy, not as selfless a sacrifice as it seemed. Since our town was so small and spread out, Mom drove us around and kept the heater cranked up high. I don't know how we would have survived otherwise.

When we were little, Mom would dress up too, though I don't remember when that ended, because with her fourth-graders, she loves every aspect of Halloween. She has hand-me-up costumes from my California cousins who have grown out of them (and since Mom is five-four, she still fits in them). My current favorite of that lot is the Pile of Leaves costume. I don't think Dad ever dressed up.

The blizzard of the current age is the 1991 Halloween Blizzard, which ranks as number four on the Minnesota weather events of the century, the storm that set most of the records for snowfall in the state, yet I retain no memories of it. The storm system also affected the 1991 Perfect Storm, which merged a nor'easter with a hurricane over the East Coast, sinking the *Andrea Gail*—a moment in time eventually represented by a book and a movie— and though the storm systems were separate from each other, the Perfect Storm influenced the track and severity of the Halloween Blizzard. These are the connections and influences we cannot see, but what would the storm tracks of our lives look like if we had tools to see these invisibles?

What happens when these important moments fade? Do we acquire new knowledge to fill the gaps? Does the Children's Blizzard exist only in poetry and books, as if we invented the story to entertain us? What happens when those who remember the Armistice Day Blizzard are gone, and those who remain wonder what Armistice Day commemorated? If we learned from the Children's Blizzard that predictions are only as good as those who make them—and distribute them—and if the Armistice Day Blizzard taught us that the National Weather Service needs to communicate better with its various branches, and if the Halloween Blizzard reminded us that we live in a place that holds its historical memories longer and better than we do, then where do we go from here? Maybe the larger question is, *What value is historical memory?* The Irish poet Michael Coady writes, "It is in remembering / little by little / that we are allowed to forget" ("One Another"). For all that I believe in the importance of historical memory and that we put ourselves into great physical danger when we do not know what the bedrock tells, when we ignore what has happened and plow ourselves into another Dust Bowl, I also believe that historical memory can be too much weight. Sometimes we need to forget in order to add new memories to the path.

How do we come to know what it means to live in *this* place on *this* day?

On this day, it means bundling up our most precious little girl in the warmest clothes she owns, watching her hop down the sidewalk, enthusiastically enough to make her ears flop, in the late October, late afternoon darkness, wondering if that will be enough to teach her what she needs to know. Maybe next year she will want to be a ballerina. Maybe next year there will be snow for Halloween.

The Weight of Water

July 2006

Two months before my maternal grandfather died in his sleep, I spent a month with my parents, forty-five miles away from where I grew up in northern Minnesota, and each week of that month I spent a night with my grandparents. While the town I grew up in doesn't call to me, the Cabin remains our family's emotional home, that small, two-bedroom cabin on a shallow lake, with a picture window that looks out onto thick trees that obscure the water when they are not pruned back. On one of those nights, my mother and I pulled into a driveway of complete darkness. My watch read 10:30. I muttered my bad-tempered irritation with Gram not leaving the garage light on for us, as she had failed to do the week before as well, so we had to walk up to the house blind. We had driven through a delicious thunderstorm to get here, and the air was still thick with it, a storm still tangible enough to chew. The humidity was as dense as the darkness.

A light appears in the doorway. Gram stands on the stoop in her flannel nightgown, her hair wrapped in pink foam curlers and covered in a red kerchief, an oil lantern in her hand. My mother and I stare in disbelief.

"The power is out," Gram calls.

"Oh," we say, shaking our heads. That explains the garage light and the lantern, but not the flannel, especially if her air conditioner isn't working.

In our world, the Cabin is a proper noun. Grandpa is eighty-six, she is eighty-two. Their health is deteriorating, but they remain lightning sharp. Not physically strong enough to go down to the lake to get a bucket of water to flush the toilet—since the power is out—Gram hands my mother a flashlight and hands me a five-gallon bucket. The rain had stopped, but lightning still flashed its reflection in the lake, and thunder still shook the treetops. We use the neighbor's dock, since we don't have one, and I kneel to fill the bucket. Forty pounds of water—it never ceases to amaze me how something so clear can weigh so much. We giggle our way back up the hill to the Cabin, uncharacteristic for both of us, and we blame our reaction on the lateness of the hour and the sheer absurdity of the moment. My mother points the flashlight at my feet and tells me, helpfully, not to trip. We look up, and Gram is standing just outside the basement door. We blink a few times before we realize that she is standing in the light from the house.

"The power is back on," she says.

We follow Gram up the stairs, to where Grandpa is sitting in his customary chair, looking out the picture window toward the lake. My mother and I sit, and even though it is late, we chat a little. They waited up for us. Had the power not been out, had they been able to watch the end of the Twins game, they might have gone to bed. My grandmother is notorious for giving up on losing teams early in a game. If the Twins are behind by a run in the sixth inning, she will go to bed. The family calls such a maneuver "a Phyllis" after her name.

Then my grandfather starts to talk. He never does this. My grandmother is the one who is quick with a story. He never uses his voice more than he has to. He never has. It's one of his charms, of which he has many. He's on the short side, probably not more than five-six, with thick gray hair that waves when it's long, perfect hair for three little granddaughters to play Beauty Shop with. He is a quiet man, one who thinks through everything before he says it, and the result is a dry wit and what seems like absolute wisdom. Gram is the one who tells his stories. He's more likely to twinkle than to tell a story, but tonight, he's telling us about the Coast Guard.

Kermit left the farm in Clara City, Minnesota, in south-western Minnesota to go to war in 1943. He was twenty-four years old. His older brother Leonard was drafted, not Kermit, but the story goes that their father decided that Kermit should be the one to go. Kermit was the first of his family to graduate from high school, which Ulfert thought was a waste of time. The fact that Kermit went to college was beyond Ulfert's comprehension. From stories I have heard, I wonder if Ulfert actually cared that his younger son might be killed in the war—or if Ulfert, who was third-generation German, thought much about the war at all. When I asked my grandmother why Kermit chose the water and the Coast Guard, she told me, "Well, so he would always have a place to sleep," which I recognized as something Kermit would say. The Army wouldn't always have a place to sleep, he figured.

Kermit, during his enlisted time, served in the lighthouse system in California, and when he became an officer, sailed on the *Charlottesville* in the South Pacific, through the Panama Canal, and even across the International Date Line on his birthday. The *Charlottesville* was a Tacoma-class frigate, a convoy escort also on antisubmarine patrol. It was built in 1943, commissioned in 1944, decommissioned in 1945, and then given to the Russians. Gram has strong opinions about this handover, but my grandfather stays silent on this issue.

I can understand why he doesn't tell many of his Coast Guard stories. When he went to war, everyone he knew called him Bud, and that's the way that he signed all his letters to his mother. When he returned after four years, he signed his letters *Kermit*. He was not the same man. When he returned from war, his family told him they thought he had been *on a four-year vacation*. I can imagine his father and brother saying so, but his mother knew exactly what he had been doing. A vacation where they ate bread—but only after they had knocked most of the weevils out of it. A South Pacific vacation where his ship couldn't go too close to some of the battles because of the kamikazes. Where the Ka-Bar knife that I found on a shelf in his office at the Cabin after he died had been used for more than decoration. My grandmother reports that he never used it for its intended function, but some of the matte-black finish of the blade had been worn off while keeping it sharp. A vacation. But to a farmer, nothing but farming is considered work. After my grandfather was discharged from the Coast Guard, he taught vocational agriculture and agricultural economics, something that never sat well with his family. The only thing that mattered to them was the land. When his brother's younger son chose to continue his education and teach agriculture at the University of Washington, that meant something.

But the sea matters too. At the annual Memorial Day service at the Park Rapids High School, Grandpa was the only one to stand up when the Coast Guard hymn was played. Now he's gone, and the sea and its stories matter even more.

There is a part of me that wants to make a case for the sea being in my blood. My ancestors were not seafarers, though my genealogical research has turned up information on one William Hoadley, born 1791, who made his living trading in human lives. The entry in the family tree says this: "Went to Brazil and then to Jamaica Slave-trading." Every family tree has to have one branch that should meet a chainsaw. My maternal grandfather served in the Coast Guard during World War II, but other family military service has been in the Army or Air Force, my father retiring from the Air Force Reserves in 2000. I have spent most of my life landlocked: the first twenty-two years in Minnesota, and the following years in eastern Washington State and Ohio and Nebraska. I fear drowning, a phobia likely exacerbated by the time my sister held me under water by sitting on my head. I was six; she was four.

But I grew up in the fresh water of northern Minnesota, three blocks from the beach on Lake Belle Taine, where we learned to swim in the frigid June waters before the summer had a chance to warm the lake. I spent every last day of elementary school at the Headwaters of the Mississippi River, walking across the slippery boulders until I could do it without getting wet. Our fifth-grade field trip was to Duluth, on the shores of Lake Superior, where I first learned of the *Edmund Fitzgerald* and that the sea—even the freshwater sea—is a nasty bitch.

The Great Lakes are considered to be some of the most dangerous waters in the world to cross by boat. Though they are called lakes, the five Great Lakes are, more accurately, inland seas. Weather patterns on the lakes are such that sailors consider the month of November cursed, calling the weather the Witch of November. During the Great Storm of 1913, a convergence of two storm systems produced hurricane-force winds, still considered the deadliest storm on the Great Lakes. The Witch wreaked something beyond havoc, just because she could. According to Michael Schumacher in *November's Fury,* "Twelve boats had sunk, thirty-one had been grounded on rocks or beaches, and dozens more were severely damaged." More than two hundred fifty were killed, and four of the ships have never been found.

The Witch, she's a nasty one—and she doesn't haunt the Great Lakes alone.

Just because the lakes are not salt doesn't mean they are tame.

Whether the lakes are filled with fresh water or salt water makes no difference to those the Lakes have claimed. Humans cannot breathe either one. Estimates of how many ships have sunk there range from six thousand to eight thousand, with a possible loss of life of nearly thirty thousand people. It is not a surprise that some consider the Great Lakes haunted, or even cursed. The Three Sisters is a Lake Superior phenomenon in which a ship is hit by three sequential large waves, allowing no time for recovery. Estimates of how much water hits the ship are in the five-thousand-ton range. Rogue waves have long been considered a maritime myth, stories that only serve to explain the unexplainable. Only recently has science been able to confirm what sailors have spoken of for hundreds of years.

The sinking of the *Edmund Fitzgerald* in November 1975 makes no logical sense because we have come to rely on technology to tell us what we should know rather than trusting those who knew that ship, knew Lake Superior. It is the modern age of weather technology. We have radar; we have satellites. That made no difference to the *Edmund Fitzgerald* and those who sailed her. No difference at all.

Over the days of November 9–11, 1975, the Witch threw herself a hissy fit of grandest proportions. The Soo Locks reported winds of 100 miles per hour. When the storm was over, the *Edmund Fitzgerald* was the largest ship ever lost on the Great Lakes, and twenty-nine sailors lost with it. The *Fitzgerald* was carrying 26,000 tons of iron ore. She set off from Superior, Wisconsin, and after losing her radar she tried to follow the *Arthur M. Anderson,* though the *Fitzgerald* was sixteen miles ahead of the *Anderson* when she sank. Squalls, bad weather in November—all Great Lakes sailors are familiar with such conditions. What was not familiar, what could not be explained, was the loss of the *Fitzgerald.*

When the squall was over, ten minutes later, the *Fitzgerald* was gone. Completely gone. She had vanished as if she had never been there in the first place; there was no sign that her crew had ever existed. There were no lifeboats put off, no distress signals, no survivors, no bodies. Most didn't think the lack of bodies was too strange because Lake Superior has a nasty habit of never giving up her dead. But *ten minutes?*—that needs an explanation.

When divers explored the *Fitzgerald,* they found she had broken in half, like the *Titanic* had. Some speculate that the *Fitzgerald* hit a shoal. Some believe her design was flawed, that her age and wear made her weak. Some speculate that she had been hit by Three Sisters waves. Some speculate that she had been hit by a rogue wave, a piece of sailor lore that has recently been scientifically documented. The lack of bodies recovered gave rise to the ubiquitous alien abduction theory, which is about as plausible as anything else. Three different organizations conducted investigations into the *Fitzgerald,* and each came up with a different answer. In any case, the years since have not provided definitive answers, and we will probably never know exactly what happened, since the site is in Canadian waters and has been designated a burial site. No further diving or study is allowed.

We still talk about curses on the ship and curses of the month of November—and the Witch of November herself—to explain the loss of the *Fitzgerald*. We fetishize the *Fitzgerald,* to the point where high-end stained glass art and paintings of the ship, sitting right next to tiny replicas, are a solid source of income around the North Shore of Lake Superior. Stories are all we have to make sense of what cannot be explained. We cannot be comfortable with the empty spaces.

Some say that when the *Fitzgerald* was launched, she was thirteen feet longer than her nearest competitor—and that thirteen feet, they say, cursed the ship. They say that the wine bottle used to christen the ship didn't break. They say that is further proof of a curse, especially since christenings are considered good luck for sailors. If she was cursed from the beginning, then her mysterious loss was a foregone conclusion—and nothing the sailors or the weather forecasters could have done would have saved her.

If that's the case, if there's nothing that anybody could have done to combat the forces of the Fates, then there's no sense stewing about the *what ifs* or *what might have beens*. The populace needs an explanation that comforts them, which usually means blaming something specific for disasters, for people not returning home. We need answers to the unanswerable questions—and so we use these curses, these superstitions, to counteract our grief, as if that would somehow give us peace. Religion almost never offers the comfort we need. If there is nothing we could have done, then we can breathe easier, knowing that we are not to blame for not trying harder.

Part of it stems from a natural fear of water. Humans are made for land, not water. The land is solid, more controllable than the sea—which may explain my grandfather's family's distancing themselves from my grandfather's sea service. They couldn't understand it, so they avoided it. These stories turn the water into a morality tale: *Do this and you will be all right. Fail to do so and you will learn what sailors before you have learned.*

In 1913, the Revenue Cutter Service, forerunner of the Coast Guard, began to patrol the "iceberg alley." The first Safety of Life at Sea conference, an international coalition, assembled in 1914. The Ice Patrol website claims that this type of alliance would not have happened without a disastrous catalyst like the sinking of the *Titanic*. Every year, except in wartime, the International Ice Observation and Ice Patrol Service has been maintained by the U.S. Coast Guard, supported by thirteen nations. The Ice Patrol website reports that there have been no losses of life from iceberg collisions with ships that heeded Ice Patrol's warnings.

Heeded the warnings?

Or followed the superstitions?

Does it matter?

Every April 15, the Ice Patrol lays a wreath over the final resting place of the *Titanic* and watches it disappear beneath the waves.

On a stormy July night in 2006, my grandfather tells the story of a storm that nearly capsized their ship—an event he slept through. The swells were monstrous, and the *Charlottesville* hit one broadside, tipping the ship to a 45-degree angle, where they stayed for half an hour. The ship could handle a 48-degree tilt, he said.

Luck? Coincidence?

We are not willing to accept the reality of accidents, good or bad. Someone has to be blamed or credited, so all kinds of coincidences and superstitions float on top of and sit on the bottom of the Great Lakes and the Seven Seas. The Fates sit somewhere, having tea with the Witch of November and the Three Sisters, perhaps wanting a bit of company, cooking up mischief.

We compensate by creating stories to fill the empty spaces where we think stories should be. Women on board a ship make the sea angry, but a naked woman on board brings good luck—hence so many naked figureheads. It is unlucky to have anything to do with a Friday, since that was the day Christ was crucified. The British Navy gamely tried to disprove this superstition:

They laid the keel of a ship on a Friday, named it the *HMS Friday,* launched it on a Friday, sent it to sea on a Friday. Neither the ship nor crew were ever heard from again. Then there were three ships named *Stone* sailing on the Great Lakes, each lost on October 12: *William Stone* (1901), *Ella G. Stone* (1918), and *George Stone* (1919).

Is it coincidence that Violet Jessup survived the sinking of the *Titanic,* the sinking of the *Britannic,* and the collision of the *Olympic* with the warship *Hawke?* Did someone on the *Britannic* do something wrong, and that is why a few people were chopped to pieces as they tried to escape the sinking ship? Or was Violet the reason why two ships sank and one nearly did?

Did someone knock on wood aboard the *Charlottesville,* and that is why the ship didn't capsize? Because someone followed all the correct, superstitious protocol, that is why the *Charlottesville* survived the kamikazes?

I want to know what my land-bred grandfather thought about these events and if he and his fellow crew members gave any thought to curses and superstitions. Did my very level-headed, grounded-in-his-faith grandfather carry lucky tokens? I pick up my cell phone to call him before I remember he is dead. I sit for a while, phone in hand, wrapped in the scratchy wool of unanswered questions.

There is nothing to explain why my grandfather lived as long as he did. He was diagnosed with leukemia in 1973 on his twenty-fifth wedding anniversary. His Parkinson's was diagnosed in the 1980s. He had both knees replaced, one of which attracted a staph infection that nearly killed him. His leukemia caused his spleen to enlarge—I remember this, Christmas 1990—and Gram took him to his scheduled appointment at the Mayo Clinic a day early, which was lucky, because she took him to the ER that night, and they rushed him into surgery. If the spleen had burst, it would have killed him. In 2002, he fell and cracked his pelvis. He survived hernia surgeries, bowel resections, bladder infections. In 2003, he and my father were driving back from the Christmas concert where my sisters were going to college (Mom and Gram were driving back the next day), and my grandfather wasn't feeling well. Dad took him to the ER and they found a ruptured abdominal aortic aneurysm. It had been seeping slowly enough that it didn't kill him, but the ensuing surgery kills 90 percent of patients, and survival rates for those over eighty years of age is almost zero. Grandpa was eighty-five. Was it luck or something else that caused my grandparents to go to Mayo a day early? That caused my father to take my grandfather home early? In 2006, he suffered another ruptured abdominal aortic aneurysm and survived the surgery again, but the day before he was to be released from the hospital, he died in his sleep. We don't know how to understand these things, so we tell the stories. The stories become what matters.

After Kermit graduated from the Coast Guard Academy and was commissioned an officer, he spent time in New Orleans. The Danish had sent the *Danmark,* a full-rigged sailing ship, to the United States to train sailors and to keep it out of German hands. Because my grandfather was "such a little guy," as my grandmother says—and the photographs of him from the time put him about five-six and skinny—he and a friend volunteered to take care of the sails at the top of the masts. I wonder what they talked about up there, the responsibility of tying those knots just right, what would happen if they failed, how many sailors' lives would be in their hands. I wonder what he thought of being in a place where his size and intelligence were respected rather than being on the farm where he was bullied by his father and brother, in a time before "abuse" was more than simply how children were raised. As far as I know, I never heard my grandfather speak an unkind word about his father or brother. Only in reading between the lines do I get a sense of how it must really have been for Kermit to grow up in that house, small and slight, loving music and learning, even as he did his chores without complaining, returning to help out at the farm without being asked long after he had left. I can understand why my land-raised grandfather might have chosen the military option that was the furthest thing from what he knew, because the farming he knew was not something he wanted to remember.

Before the academy, Kermit was stationed in California in three different lighthouses, responsible for keeping ships safe and off the rocks at his feet. I wonder what stories he heard while they wiped the lamps and replaced bulbs, stories of ships lost before the lighthouse was built, ships lost after the lighthouse was built, terrible and wonderful storms, ghost ships and ghost sailors and unfinished business, cursed to sail the seas, walk the land until Judgment Day. I imagine that my grandfather did not tell those stories because he was not one who talked much, and he would have considered superstitions something that went against the idea of his faith. I remember back to that dark night at the Cabin, with Gram standing on the step holding a lantern to guide us home.

What does matter is that we tell these stories, generation after generation, not just the stories of the ships themselves but the stories that keep the ship and her sailors safe—or did not keep her sailors safe. The stories counteract the grief of those not lost to the waves, to apply reason to the unexplainable. I wonder about friends my grandfather must have lost in the war, the ones who did not survive the kamikazes, the ones who were prisoners of war, the ones who also came home and did not talk about what had happened to them.

We blame the stories of the *Mary Celeste* on curses. She was a ship that seemed to be cursed from the day of her christening as the *Amazon* in 1861. So much had gone wrong with her that by 1872 she had been sold and her name changed to *Mary Celeste* in hopes of distracting the dark forces at work.

In November 1872, she put off for Genoa, Italy, under the captainship of Benjamin Briggs. In early December 1872, the *Mary Celeste* was spotted off the Azores with no sign of life on board. Food was in the galley, some of it served. Breakfast was still waiting in the captain's cabin. The last date in the captain's log was November 25, and he did not indicate that anything was wrong. No one has ever been able to explain what happened to those people or how the *Mary Celeste* stayed on her course to Genoa with no one aboard for five hundred miles.

Given her history, it is not a stretch to consider the *Mary Celeste* cursed. Bad weather was ruled out as a possible reason for abandoning the ship, though recent speculation about a seaquake has garnered attention. Some wondered about a mutiny, but there was no sign of any kind of struggle. A curse, logically assumed from the *Mary Celeste*'s history, was an explanation survivors could live with. A curse probably reaffirmed for them the awesome power of the Almighty and the active presence of the Devil. There wasn't anything they could have done to save her, even if they had tried. Forces more powerful than themselves were at work. How can one compete with that? So the survivors can live with not trying.

In one of his rare moments of storytelling—rare in that there was no prompting—my grandfather once told me about being on the edge of a monsoon. He was up on the bridge at night, sixty feet above the waterline, and he sees what looks like a fire in the distance. He calls for another opinion—yes, it is a fire. They set their course for the fire, and the seas are picking up. All the crew of the *Charlottesville* is ordered belowdecks because the waves that crash over the ship are enough to drown a man. The fire turns out to be a Japanese fishing boat, too small to be able to survive the monsoon, sending a distress signal by setting a fire on their boat to attract attention. With swells up to thirty or forty feet, the *Charlottesville* launches a boat to rescue the crew. It is dark. The winds are sharp enough to whip the skin. The sea is hungry, out for blood, meat. And yet they go, into swells that are as high as the bridge. When the crew is rescued and brought on deck, the captain of the Japanese boat orders his men to lie down on the deck, facedown, their hands on their heads. They are expecting to be executed on the spot. Instead, the crew of the *Charlottesville* takes the Japanese below to feed them. The fishermen are let off at the first Japanese port they reach.

After the war, the *Charlottesville* is decommissioned and given to the Russians, who return her when her lease is up in 1949. In 1953, she is acquired by the Japanese, who rename her *Matsu,* and I wonder if any Japanese who sail on the *Matsu* remember that night on the *Charlottesville.* I wonder what stories they tell their grandchildren, about how they were rescued and why they were spared. I wonder what stories they do not tell.

Joan Didion famously titled her book, "We tell ourselves stories in order to live." Tim O'Brien wrote in *The Things They Carried,* "Stories are for joining the past to the future. Stories are for those late hours in the night when you can't remember how you got from where you were to where you are. Stories are for eternity, when memory is erased, when there is nothing to remember except the story." My grandfather's war stories aren't like O'Brien's war stories, and they aren't like my paternal grandfather's war stories. Kermit's war stories were not for telling. Kermit's war stories are the stories he could barely bring himself to tell, the ones that were not in search of meaning and understanding but simply about something happening. He never editorialized, never speculated about what other people might have been thinking or feeling. His stories were things he could understand, as far as he could understand them. His stories were about finding something as solid as the land he left in southwestern Minnesota, the land he understood but the people he didn't, his way of finding what mattered and staying there.

There are moments at Third Crow Wing, when the wind off the water is just right, when it's impossible to tell if the sound is wind in the trees or rain in the leaves. This morning, not a leaf is moving out the big picture window to the west, the window that looks toward the lake, but I can hear something moving out there that catches me off guard, makes me wonder what I am hearing. It is never quiet here, but the only birdsong I can identify—even as a born and bred Minnesotan—is the loon calls that wake me in the morning and send me to sleep after dusk. Somehow, I don't mind that they are the only sounds I can put a face to. I don't mind that there are words beyond my hearing, stories beyond my understanding, here in this place.

The Japanese name for the *Charlottesville*—the *Matsu*—translates to "pine tree," but the word also translates to the verb "to wait." Something that I didn't understand before slips into place, back into the spaces between the white pine needles at Third Crow Wing, to the Kermit Trees and my grandmother's voice teaching us that for every tree that fell or had to be cut down, they planted new trees. We will teach my niece and nephew their numbers by counting the rows of branches because that is how old the tree is. We will teach them to recognize a Norway pine when they are old enough. And we will transplant those Kermit Trees to a spot where they will have enough sun to grow, we will push a stake into the ground to keep each one safe, and maybe one day Cora and Henry will teach the next generation how to read the trees at Third Crow Wing.

ACKNOWLEDGMENTS

I am grateful to the editors of the journals in which some of these essays first appeared: *River Teeth, Sycamore Review, North Dakota Quarterly, Natural Bridge, Silk Road Literary Review, Fugue, South Dakota Review,* and *Weber: The Contemporary West.*

Special thanks to my mentors and friends who guided these essays through their various incarnations: Jonis Agee, Joy Castro, John Keeble, Jonathan Johnson, Scott Olsen, and Jim Rogers.

Thank you, also, to Erik Anderson and the wonderful team at the University of Minnesota Press.

KAREN BABINE is assistant professor of English at Concordia College in Moorhead, Minnesota. Her essays have been published in *River Teeth, Ascent, Natural Bridge, Sycamore Review,* and *Fugue*. She is the editor of *Assay: A Journal of Nonfiction Studies.*